Darkest Secrets of Persuasion & Seduction Masters

How to Protect Yourself and Turn the Power to Good

(Text and Workbook)

from YourBodySoulandProsperity.com

Tom Marcoux

Executive Coach

Spoken Word Strategist

Speaker-Author of 36 books

A QuickBreakthrough Publishing Edition

Copyright © 2013 Tom Marcoux Media, LLC
ISBN: 0615783422
ISBN-13: 978-0615783420

All rights reserved. No part of this book may be reproduced or transmitted in any form by any means electronic or mechanical, including photocopying, recording or by any information storage and retrieval system without written permission from the publisher.

More copies are available from the publisher with the imprint QuickBreakthrough Publishing. For more information about this book contact: tomsupercoach@gmail.com

This book was developed and written with care. Names and details were modified to respect privacy.

Disclaimer: The author and publisher acknowledge that each person's situation is unique, and that readers have full responsibility to seek consultations with health, financial, spiritual and legal professionals. The author and publisher make no representations or warranties of any kind, and the author and publisher shall not be liable for any special, consequential or exemplary damages resulting, in whole or in part, from the reader's use of, or reliance upon, this material.:

Other Books by Tom Marcoux:
- What the Rich Don't Say about Getting Rich
- Time Management Secrets the Rich Won't Tell You
- Discover Your Enchanted Prosperity
- Emotion-Motion Life Hacks ... for More Success and Happiness
- Relax Your Way Networking
- Connect: High Trust Communication for Your Success
- Darkest Secrets of Persuasion and Seduction Masters
- Darkest Secrets of Charisma
- Darkest Secrets of Negotiation Masters
- Darkest Secrets of the Film and TV Industry Every Actor Should Know
- Darkest Secrets of Making a Pitch to the Film and Television Industry
- Darkest Secrets of Film Directing

Praise for *Time Management Secrets the Rich Won't Tell You* and Tom Marcoux:

• "Learn how to defend yourself against manipulation!" – Dr. JoAnn Dahlkoetter, author, *Your Performing Edge* and Coach to CEOs and Olympic Gold Medalists
• "Tom gives you useful countermeasures to protect you from being darkly manipulated." – David Barron, co-author of *Power Persuasion*

Praise for Tom Marcoux's Other Work:
• "Concerned about networking situations? Get *Relax Your Way Networking*. Success is built on high trust relationships. Master Coach Tom Marcoux reveals secrets to increase your influence."
– Greg S. Reid, Author, *Think and Grow Rich Series*
• "In Tom Marcoux's *Now You See Me*, the powerful and easy-to-use ideas can make a big difference in your business and your personal relationships." – Allen Klein, author of *You Can't Ruin My Day*
• "Marcoux's book *10 Seconds to Wealth* focuses on how each of us have divine gifts that we need to understand and use to be our best when the crucial '10 seconds' occur.... He identifies the divine gifts and shares how these gifts can help us create what we want in our lives, and the wealth we want." – Linda Finkle, author of *Finding The Fork In The Road: The Art of Maximizing the Potential of Business Partnerships*
• "In *Darkest Secrets of Persuasion and Seduction Masters: How to Protect Yourself and Turn the Power to Good*, learn useful countermeasures to protect you from being darkly manipulated."
– David Barron, co-author, *Power Persuasion*
• "In *Be Heard and Be Trusted*, Tom's advice on how to remain true to yourself and establish authentic rapport with clients is both insightful and reality based. He [shows how] to establish oneself as a credible expert."
- Arthur P. Ciaramicoli, Ed.D., Ph.D., author *The Curse of the Capable*
• "In *Reduce Clutter, Enlarge Your Life*, Marcoux will help you get rid of the physical and mental clutter occupying precious space in your life. You'll reclaim wasted energy, lower your stress, and find time for new opportunities." – Laura Stack, author of *Execution IS the Strategy*

Visit Tom's blog: www.BeHeardandBeTrusted.com

Tom Marcoux

CONTENTS*

Dedication and Acknowledgments	6
Book I: Darkest Secrets of Persuasion Masters	7
Book II: Darkest Secrets of Seduction Masters	44
Book III: Make a Great First Impression and Turn Seduction-Power to Good (Part 1)	75
Book III: Make a Great First Impression and Turn Seduction-Power to Good (Part 2)	109
Book IV: Use Strategies to Make Yourself Stronger (Your Defense Against Manipulators)	123
A Final Word and Springboard to Your Dreams	177
Excerpt from *Darkest Secrets of Negotiation Masters: How to Protect Yourself, Overcome Intimidation, Get Stronger and Turn the Power to Good*	178
About the Author Tom Marcoux	181
Special Offer Just for Readers of this Book	177

* This table includes highlights. This book includes even more material!

DEDICATION AND ACKNOWLEDGEMENTS

This book is dedicated to the terrific book and film consultant, and author Johanna E. Mac Leod. It is also dedicated to the other team members. Thanks to Linda L. Chappo and Jill Ronsley (www.SunEditWrite.com), for editing. Thanks to Danek S. Kaus and Joan Harrison for editing the new section for the Second Edition. Thanks to Shou June Lin for the book's front cover design. Thanks to Johanna E. MacLeod for the rendering of the cover for this edition. Thanks to my father, Al Marcoux, for his concern and efforts for me. Thanks to my mother, Sumiyo Marcoux, a kind, generous soul. Thank you to Higher Power. Thanks to our readers, audiences, clients, my graduate/college students and my team members of
Tom Marcoux Media, LLC.
The best to you.

Book One:
Darkest Secrets of Persuasion Masters

I never expected to write *Darkest Secrets of Persuasion and Seduction Masters: How to Protect Yourself and Turn the Power to Good.*

But I was angry and I had to stand up for you.

When I was a child, I was hurt badly. My parents could not protect me. As a young man, in one of my first business deals, I was hurt terribly.

Now, I am in my 40's, with gray in my hair, and for 27 years I have been taking action to protect people.

And now is the time for me to protect you with the Countermeasures I reveal in this book.

Every human being needs to be able to break the trance that a Manipulator creates. You need to make good decisions so you are safe and you keep growing—and you are not cut down and crippled.

This Darkest Secrets material is so intense that I first released it only with the counterbalance of my most energizing and uplifting books, *Nothing Can Stop You This Year!* and *The Hidden Power of the AND-Universe.*

An interviewer asked me: "Who can be the Manipulator?"

A co-worker, a boss, a salesperson, someone you're dating, and someone you think is a friend.

Now is the time—this very minute—for me to write this

book to protect you.

I must speak the truth.

These darkest secrets of "persuasion masters" are …

Wait a minute! Let's say it plainly: These are the darkest secrets of masters of manipulation. Throughout this book, I will call these people what they are: Manipulators.

Dictionary.com defines "manipulate" as "To influence or manage shrewdly or deviously…. To tamper with or falsify for personal gain."

In this book, we will look on a manipulator as one who deviously influences someone with no concern about that person's well-being, and who causes harm to that person.

Here is the first Darkest Secret:

Darkest Secret #1:

Manipulators Make You Hurt and Then Offer the Salve.

Manipulators would invite you to go out in the sun for hours and then sell you the salve to soothe your burns. The problem is that we don't notice that this is what they're doing.

For example, you're considering the purchase of a house. A Manipulator asks the question, "So, where would you put your TV?" This question is designed to put you into a trance.

Dictionary.com defines "trance" as "a half-conscious state, seemingly between sleeping and waking, in which ability to function voluntarily may be suspended." Let's condense this: in a trance you may not be able to function freely.

Here is the second Darkest Secret:

Darkest Secret #2:

Manipulators Put You into a Trance.

To protect yourself, you must learn to use Countermeasures to Break the Trance.

All the Countermeasures (actions you can take to break

the trance) in this book will make you stronger and more capable of protecting yourself.

Now, we'll view the third Darkest Secret:

Darkest Secret #3:

Manipulators Care Nothing for You and Human Decency: They'll lie, cheat, and do whatever they need to do so they win—but their charm masks all this.

Let's return to the example of a Manipulator selling you a house. A Manipulator does not pause for an instant to see if you can truly afford the new house. The Manipulator would neglect to mention that you will not only have your mortgage payment of $900. There will be additional costs: home repairs, property tax, water, electricity, homeowner's insurance, and more. The Manipulator only emphasizes what he or she knows you want to hear: "Look! $900 is better than the $1500 you're paying for rent, which is just going down the toilet. And the $900 is an investment."

Let's go back to **Darkest Secret #1:**

Manipulators make you hurt and then offer the salve.

The Manipulator has you feeling good about the solution (salve) and feeling bad about your current life situation.

How? A Manipulator will make you hurt through questions such as:

- What bothers you about paying $1500 a month for rent? (The Manipulator will use a derisive tone when he says the word rent.)
- What is not smart about paying rent on someone else's house instead of investing in your own house?
- How do you feel about your children walking in the neighborhood where you live now?

Do you see how these questions are designed to make you hurt enough so that you'll buy?

An interviewer asked me, "Tom, aren't these good arguments for purchasing a house?"

"What we're looking at is the intention of the influencer," I replied. "Let's look at our definition of a manipulator as one who deviously influences someone with no concern about that person's well-being, and who causes harm to that person. If the person truly cannot afford the house, he or she will be harmed by buying it. If the manipulator conceals the truth, the manipulator is doing harm. That's the important difference."

Some friends of mine are ethical and helpful real estate agents who truthfully reveal the whole situation and help the purchaser achieve her own goals.

In this book, we are talking about another type of person; that is, unethical Manipulators.

* * *

In any given moment, we need to remember the tactics Manipulators use. We will focus on the word D.A.R.K. so you can remember details easily and protect yourself from Manipulators.

D — Dangle something for nothing
A — Alert to scarcity
R — Reveal the Desperate Hot Button
K — Keep on pushing buttons

We'll begin with *Dangle something for nothing* with the next chapter.

1. **Who in your life is manipulating you?**

Chapter 2: Dangle Something for Nothing

The first method of D.A.R.K. is *Dangle Something for Nothing.*

What do conmen and conwomen do to seize your attention? They make you think you're getting a "steal."

I recently saw a documentary in which a conman on a street in England showed a toy that looked like it was dancing. This fake product was actually dancing because of a hidden, invisible thread. The conman was dangling something for nothing. The Entranced Buyer thought he was getting something worth $20 for only $5. That was the trick. The Entranced Buyer felt that he was getting $15 extra of value for his $5. What the Buyer really got was something worth nothing. Similarly, I know someone who purchased a copy of a Disney movie from a street vendor in San Francisco. She brought the copy home and it was unwatchable—and the street vendor was never seen again.

An old phrase goes, "A conman cannot con someone who is not looking for something for nothing."

How to Protect Yourself from "Dangle Something for Nothing"

Stop! Get on your cell phone and talk through the "deal" with someone you know who thinks clearly. Go home. Think about it. Do some research on the Internet. Listen to your gut feelings. If the salesman or conman is too insistent, get away from that Manipulator. Get quiet. Have a cup of water. Cool down. Break the Trance!

Break the Trance and Identify the Crucial Detail

Earlier, I mentioned that a Manipulator puts you into a

trance. An added problem is that we put ourselves into a trance. For example, as you read this, are you thinking about your right toe? Most likely not (unless you stubbed your toe recently). The point is that we only focus on a tiny percentage of what is going on in our life.

Around fifteen years ago, I caused myself trouble because I put myself into a trance. I discovered that under certain conditions, friendship can make you nearly deaf. Here's how: I was producing a song for a motion picture. A good friend was singing backup in the chorus. Because of our friendship, I wanted him to sound great. I completely missed the Crucial Detail. In this kind of situation, the Crucial Detail is that what truly counts is how the lead singer sounds! I made a song that I could not release. What a waste of time and money! I had put myself into a trance.

In any situation in which the Manipulator is "dangling something for nothing," we often fall into a trance and miss the Crucial Detail. The most important detail is not that we're saving money if we order before midnight tonight. What counts is whether the product creates a lasting, crucial benefit in our lives. And is the benefit of the product worth the cost? Some people even program themselves to make mistakes by saying, "I can't pass up a bargain." The bargain is not the Crucial Detail.

Secrets to Break the Trance

This is the process of B.R.E.A.K.S. It will help you remember the proven methods to break a trance.

B — Breathe
R — Relax
E — Envision
A — Act on aromas
K — Keep moving

S — Smile

Secret #1: Breathe

Remember Darkest Secret #1: Manipulators make you hurt and then offer the salve. The Manipulator wants to put you into a state of being that fills you with a sense of urgency and anxiety. Oh, no! I'm going to miss the sale!

Stop this highly vulnerable state. Take a deep breath. Do it now. Take a deep breath and let your belly "get fat" by filling it with air. As you breathe out, let your belly deflate. Breathe in through your nose and breathe out through your mouth. This is called belly-breathing. Repeat the actions of belly-breathing three times. Good. Now, do you feel different? Remember, when you are relaxed, you are strong.

Secret #2: Relax

You become stronger when you condition yourself to relax in the face of adversity. Researchers note that when an Olympic athlete is confronted with the most stressful moment in her life, she has prepared in advance. She has given herself ways to calm down. Two powerful methods are described in this section about B.R.E.A.K.S. One is breathing, and the other is envisioning.

A special part of relaxing is the effective use of your posture. Many of us think that we're relaxed when we slouch. However, I was taught by three physical therapists that when you sit up and align your vertebrae, you are more relaxed because your back's bone structure is naturally supporting you. Many of us discover that placing a pillow behind the lumbar-area of our back helps us sit up better. If you are sitting or standing when talking with a Manipulator, ensure that your posture is aligned. You will have more power to protect yourself.

Secret #3: Envision

Envision an image that makes you feel strong. Often, our

strongest images come from movies that we saw when we were young. Some of my clients envision being strong like Xena the Warrior Princess or Superman. One client thinks of Sean Connery as James Bond. Immediately, this client walks smoothly with poise. He feels confident. Act as if you are, and you are!

Also, envision yourself being quite aware of your surroundings. On vacation, many of us become entranced by our new surroundings. Travelers let their guard down. A conperson catches them at a weak moment. It's important to stay in the present and be alert to what's going on. Stay present with your needs, and shop around before making a large purchase. Be prepared to walk away.

Watch out for Manipulators who are slick, fast talkers. They try to get your money, and just minutes after they succeed, you realize what happened.

But this is not for you! You can remind yourself with an internal comment: "I am aware. What is really going on here?"

Secret #4: Act on Aromas

Let's notice the power of an aroma.

Smell is a potent wizard that transports you across thousands of miles and all the years you have lived. – Helen Keller

Nothing is more memorable than a smell. One scent can be unexpected, momentary and fleeting, yet conjure up a childhood summer beside a lake in the mountains. – Diane Ackerman

You need to be able to calm down within seconds. One of the fastest ways to do that is to use a favorite aroma. One of my clients has conditioned herself to calm down by smelling lavender. The process for her was to recline in a hot bath and smell lavender simultaneously. Now, the smell of lavender relaxes her limbs quickly.

Remember, when you are relaxed, you neutralize the

Manipulator's tactic to make you feel that buying something now is an urgent matter. You let go of any anxious feelings the Manipulator seeks to create in you. Use an aroma to help you feel relaxed and strong.

Secret #5: Keep Moving

A trance often transfixes or freezes us, making us still. Sometimes, the most powerful way to break a trance is to use a movement that you prepared in advance. One of my clients closes his right fist and taps it on his right thigh. In his mind, he repeats the phrase: "I am my own person!" This helps him break out of a trance induced by a Manipulator.

Another client quietly snaps her fingers near her waist. This reminds her to "snap out of it."

Secret #6: Smile

Smile when you detect a Manipulator using a manipulation method. Why? If you get angry, you become vulnerable. Remember: Manipulators make you hurt and then offer the salve.

Often when we're angry, we don't realize that beneath the anger is fear. What fear? Fear of being taken advantage of. Become strong when you identify what makes you angry.

Pull out a sheet of paper or write in your personal journal.
Write the headings of two columns.
a) What Makes Me Angry
b) What Fear Might Underlie My Anger
Write the two items next to each other.
Here is an example:
A clerk is rude to me. ===> I'm afraid that I'm worthless and not worthy of being treated with respect and kindness

The list above provides good information for you. When confronted with a Manipulator that pushes your fear buttons, you can say to yourself, "Oh! That touched my fear of losing an advantage. Okay, I feel this fear—but I am more than this fear. I am intelligent and capable."

You will feel better when you smile upon detecting a Manipulator's tactic. You will feel more in control. Researchers have shown that the act of smiling actually changes one's body chemistry. Get your body on your side.

Smile and break the trance-of-anxiety that the Manipulator attempts to use against you.

Point to Remember:

Manipulators dangle something for nothing.

Your Countermeasure:

Identify the Crucial Detail. Use these questions and statements:

- What benefit do I really want?
- Is this benefit worth the costs?
- Do I know all the costs?
- I will ask and ask until I am certain about the risks involved.
- Finally, I will contact someone I respect who is outside the area and run the situation past this trusted advisor.

How will you break a trance (with the above material)?

CHAPTER 3: ALERT TO SCARCITY

The second method of D.A.R.K. is *Alert to Scarcity*.

Have you ever been in a group situation and felt your body shudder with discomfort? In several seminars, a seminar leader says, "Fifteen hundred people are here, and only 200 seats are available for the special event." Even before the seminar leader finishes his point, people are getting up and running to the back of the room to sign up for the event, which costs thousands of dollars. The seminar leader has told us that the situation is one of scarcity. There are not enough seats! One must take action immediately or lose out forever!

Wait a minute! How many of those people who get up immediately are plants? A plant is an actor or actress who fakes extraordinary interest in the product. (Side note: Did you know that the manager of a certain big-time singer in the 40s planted girls [actresses] in the audience to scream and swoon?) Also, conmen and conwomen use plants in the infamous shell game on a city street. The con-game includes shills (planted customers).

The point here is that a Manipulator creates the perception of scarcity to inspire a feeling of urgency in you. Why? Because we become afraid when we think we're going to lose something. "No! Don't take it away!"

How to Protect Yourself from "Alert to Scarcity"

Stop. Think. Will there truly never be another chance to get this information? What are the bad consequences of you over-extending and jacking up your credit card debts? Are there really only 200 seats available? Will this seminar leader go out of business so he won't be around to hold this special event again next year?

Pay attention! Do you feel a twinge of urgency? A raging feeling of urgency? Breathe. Drink a glass of water. Talk with someone you trust. Pull out a piece of paper and write things down that answer the following questions:

Questions to Deal With Feelings of Urgency

1. What is this offer?

2. How do I feel?

3. Am I vulnerable now?

4. What am I afraid of losing?

5. Where else can I put this money? What would be good or better about that?

6. Does the seller care at all whether I get value from his product?

7. What technique is the seller using?

8. Is the product really in such short supply?

9. Have I considered other ways to get the product's benefits?

10. How might I be hurt if I go ahead with this purchase?

11. Do I know all the costs? Have I asked enough questions to get all the information I need?

12. Is the cost worth the benefits?

13. How can I be sure that I will even get those benefits?

14. How do I know if any of the salesperson's claims are true? Who told me that this offer actually provides the stated benefits?

15. Can I be sure that I can get my money back?

16. Is this offer worth my time? (My time is something I can never get back.)

When you write your answers down, you might surprise yourself. "Do I really think this? That doesn't make sense. Look! I've let this Manipulator make me scared of losing something."

An interviewer asked, "Don't many of us think things through quickly? I don't know if I would go through such a list of questions—or even remember them."

"If you're going to a seminar or an open house, bring a copy of your questions in your pocket. Then you will have the tools to be stronger," I replied.

Focus on Intuition versus Fear

Some of my clients have said, "But I had an intuition that I needed to attend that special event." This brings up a crucial distinction about our feelings and what may be true intuition.

Intuition includes feelings that help you stretch and grow.

Fear, on the other hand, includes feelings that make you contract and withdraw or hide to protect yourself.

The problem is that some of us allow certain fears to blind us so we don't take appropriate action. In the book, *The Gift of Fear*, author Gavin De Becker points out that we need to stay aware and listen to ourselves. For example, if a woman feels uneasy about entering an elevator with a particular man—she should honor her intuition in this matter and stay off that elevator. Unfortunately, some women discount their feelings of dread and tell themselves, "Oh, you're just being silly. You'll look stupid refusing to get on that elevator." Some of these individuals end up dead.

Here's the point. For years, I have been studying and writing about intuition. The way we can effectively work with our intuition is by making space for our intuition. We do this by sitting quietly with our feelings. We must seek to take more time with our intuition. We can do this by taking a piece of paper and pausing to answer questions, such as:

Questions that Help Your Intuition Speak Up

1. What can I gain here?
2. How would I grow from this experience?
3. Can I be hurt here?
4. Do the costs outweigh the benefits of this product/service?
5. Do I know all the costs?

6. What questions do I need to ask so I am well-informed?
7. Is the salesperson "playing" my fears?
8. What would it cost me if I missed this opportunity?
9. Is this really an opportunity?
10. How else can I gain benefits like these?
11. How can I create more space for my intuition?
12. How about if I say, "Let me sleep on it"?
13. Is this a situation for: If in doubt, leave it out?

14. Can I go to a positive friend (one not mired in the habits of fear) and get her intuitive feelings about the offer? I will note my feelings that come up when I hear her impressions.

In many reported cases, people have listened to their intuition and gained terrific results. A number of people have said, "I felt it was important for me to go to that event." (And at that event, these proactive people met someone who later helped them get a lucky break.) Often these successful people consider themselves lucky. Becoming skilled in making space for and listening to our intuition can help us become lucky, too.

Point to Remember:

Manipulators say the situation is one of scarcity. They get you to feel fear and a sense of urgency.

Your Countermeasure:

Pause. Make space for your intuition. On a piece of paper, write down your answers to Questions that Help Your Intuition Speak Up. Or speak with a trusted advisor and take notes about what you say in response to the Questions that Help Your Intuition Speak Up. This method helps us to discover our real thoughts and feelings—those that are below the surface—about a situation. Many of us find that we become "lucky" when we listen to our intuition.

How will you make space for your intuition?

CHAPTER 4: REVEAL THE DESPERATE HOT BUTTON

The third method of D.A.R.K. is *Reveal the Desperate Hot Button.*

The Manipulator is going to try everything to get you to reveal your Desperate Hot Button. I'm not talking about a hot button like: "I want a cherry tree in the backyard just like one we had when I was a child." Certainly, this identifies something you really want. But this is not a subconscious desire that oozes desperation, because you could buy a house without a cherry tree and plant one later.

Your Desperate Hot Button rides in your subconscious mind. It is the material you don't reveal to yourself. Details like:

1) I was a geek in high school. I want to show those people that I'm as good as—No! I'm better than they are! (This is why some people get a trophy-spouse.)

2) My father beat me. No one will do that again! That's why I lift weights and take karate lessons.

3) I was attacked as a child. That's why I have this layer of fat around me. It's protection. But I feel like a disgusting piece of garbage. The entire culture says, "You're a fat pig."

4) "God expects much," so I'm never good enough. I'm never nice enough … helpful enough … strong enough … productive enough … holy enough … lovable enough.

The Manipulator will ask you questions that are designed to uncover what your Desperate Hot Button is. Remember, the Manipulator has no right to muck around with your subconscious mind!

How to Protect Yourself from Revealing Your Desperate Hot Button

Stop! Right now, open a personal journal or select a piece of paper. What are your desperate hot buttons? Write them down. The clue to what they are lies in the answer to this question: "When and how has anyone hurt you?"

When I was in grammar school, I walked up to a girl and asked, "May I walk you home?" She replied, "What for?" in front of her sister. I ran all the way home, lost my house keys and found myself in big trouble. So guess what became my desperate hot button? Well, one thing was the sense that I had to achieve and be effective so people would take me seriously.

For example, my sweetheart complains about all the books in our home. I tell her that I have read 74 books in one year. In effect, knowledge has become a form of armor for me.

My focus on knowledge could make me vulnerable to any seminar leader who tries to convince me that he has exceptional knowledge that could help me run my three companies more effectively. But here's the good news! I know what my Desperate Hot Button is, and I can take evasive action.

Before I share with you the methods of evasive action, let's make sure you identify your Desperate Hot Buttons.

Write a list on a sheet of paper or in your personal journal:

Your Desperate Hot Buttons
a) What hurt you in the past?
b) How are you vulnerable now?

Write your answers to a) and b) immediately next to each other. And write six pairs of answers.

Now that you have written down your list, you have power. You know how someone can reach in, tweak your heart and get you to do things. Now that you know, you can stop your knee-jerk reaction.

How do you stop the knee-jerk reaction? You reframe the vulnerable point and embed this in your mind. I call this embedding the reframe. By reframe, I mean change how you look at something. I'll further describe the process of reframing in the context of Strong Subconscious Methods.

Use Strong Subconscious Methods to Protect Yourself

Strong Subconscious Methods are more effective than merely reading and nodding our heads at good ideas.

Strong Subconscious Methods help us gain instant access to an empowering idea and compelling emotion, so we take effective action.

Embedding the Reframe

With my clients, I use the process of embedding the reframe. We embed the reframe by identifying emotion-triggering words. For me, the words "many options" are helpful. For example, I can reframe past rejection and focus on the fact that I now have many options—many potential clients, friends or opportunities. Some psychologists understand reframing as looking at the situation to see if any other meaning can be applied.

Strong Subconscious Methods Go Beyond Words

With one particular client, I went beyond words. I had him connect the words hidden power with making a fist and placing it over his heart.

Begin by finding emotion-triggering words. Now, write the following list in your personal journal:

Gain Power When You Reframe a Desperate Hot Button
a) What hurt you in the past?
b) How are you vulnerable now?
c) How can you "reframe" the vulnerable point?

Set up three columns and place your answers to a), b) and c) immediately next to each other.

Here is an example:

Girl rejected me when I was a grammar school boy. ==> I need to use knowledge to protect myself and my team members. ==> My phrase: I have many options to gain knowledge to help my company.

Identifying ways to reframe how you look at vulnerable points is helpful. This is the first step. The next step is crucial: you need to gain access to your emotions and use those emotions to take you to empowering action. You need to activate your subconscious mind to use the insights you listed above.

Having a good idea is not enough. Taking action with the idea—by reflex—is where the power originates.

Now we focus on three methods (parts of Strong Subconscious Methods) for adding emotion that empowers positive action.

Three Strong Subconscious Methods to Add Emotion and Take Powerful Action

People tend to have different styles of absorbing input:
a) visual,
b) auditory, and
c) kinesthetic (touch).

Method #1: Visual—Use Visualization to Create Empowering Emotions

For many people, the way to break a pattern of thinking or feeling is to use visualization. Here is a process based on research and methodologies, including Neuro-Linguistic

Programming.

This process uses two particular moments from your past:
- a painful moment
- a good moment when you did well.

To make this clear, here is an example.

1) Sarah remembers a particularly painful rejection. A prospective customer said, "That sounds stupid. I don't want that product." She holds an image of this painful situation in her mind. She sees the situation as if she is looking at it through her eyes.

2) Next, Sarah remembers a time when she was at her best while making a sales presentation. She not only got the order but actually gained a larger order than she expected. She holds this triumphant image in her mind.

3) Now, Sarah recalls the painful image of rejection, and she makes the painful image turn black and white in her imagination. Next, she makes the black and white image become smaller and smaller. This process is designed to make the image lose its grip on you.

4) Then, Sarah has the Positive Image of her triumphant moment shatter the small black and white image, until the Positive Image is huge, in full color, and it fills her mind's eye.

This is a powerful process because when done effectively, it makes the old "programming" disappear. The old programming is powerfully overwritten (like when you save a new computer file over an old draft of the file). With the new programming, you can take positive action.

* * *

Now you can try the process yourself, using
- a painful moment...and...
- a good moment in which you did well.

1) Hold an image of the painful situation in mind. See the

situation as if you are looking at it through your eyes.

2) Now, recall the image of the time when you did well.

3) Look at the painful image and turn it black and white in your imagination. Then, make the black and white image become smaller and smaller.

4) Now, have the Positive Image of your triumphant moment shatter the small black and white image until the Positive Image is huge, in full color, and it fills your mind's eye.

My clients have reported feeling better and hopeful.

Method #2: Auditory—Use Lyrics and Music to Create Empowering Emotions

Some people respond best to music and lyrics. They are often referred to as auditory people.

My client Amanda is vulnerable to rejection. If she wants to reframe rejection as "a temporary no," just having an intellectual idea or rationalization is not strong enough. She needs to make her idea memorable and powerful enough to move her emotions.

Her choice was to transform the idea into the lyrics of an original rap song:

"It's just a temp

A temp

A temporary no."

You, too, can identify positive words and add them to music. Research shows that words set to music can be nearly impossible to forget. For example, many people remember commercial jingles from their childhood, such as:

a) Double-mint, double-mint gum

b) It's the real thing. (Coca-Cola)

c) I'm a Pepper. (Dr. Pepper)

You could make your own memorable and powerful jingle.

Method #3: Kinesthetic—Use a Movement to Create Empowering Emotions

My client Sam has played the piano since he was five years old. To switch into an empowered state of being, he positions the fingers of his right hand into a C Major chord on the piano. He presses his fingers down quickly as if he were playing the notes. In his mind, he hears the uplifting chord along with his own lyrics: "Yes! I'm stronger than that!"

Using a movement is especially powerful for people who respond well to kinesthetic (touch) input. These people make comments like "It just didn't feel right" or "I knew it; I had a feeling in my gut."

In summary, we need to add emotion to a good idea or we'll stay in the dark place of Desperate Hot Buttons.

The Three Methods I have just shared with you can help you heal your Desperate Hot Buttons. These methods are components of the Strong Subconscious Methods.

* * *

Now that you have identified your vulnerable areas, or Desperate Hot Buttons, here is a powerful Countermeasure: Do not answer every question.

How to Avoid Answering Questions that Reveal Your Desperate Hot Buttons

Using methods to avoid answering a question is evasive action. Remember, just because a salesperson asks a question, you do not have an obligation to answer it.

Use any one of these options, or combine them, or modify them:

1. Pleasantly reply, "Nope. I'm not going there right now."

2. Say, "I'm not sure. I'm going to think about it."

3. If someone asks, "Don't you know?" just smile and say, "Yes."

4. Be silent. Say nothing. Smile. Eventually, the salesperson will start talking. Many can't take the silence.

5. After a period of your silence, the salesperson may say, "So, you're not going to answer that?" You reply, "What's next?"

6. Say, "That's a good question." Then remain silent.

7. Use the Politician's Twist. Say, "That's a good question. It reminds me that the real thing we're looking for is ..."

8. Ask a question immediately, such as, "Now, why would you want to know that?"

Point to Remember:

Manipulators push you to reveal your Desperate Hot Buttons.

Your Countermeasure:

Learn to use evasive action, which is using the eight methods outlined above to avoid answering intrusive questions. Also, use the Three Methods to add emotion and take powerful action. This can be the start of healing your Desperate Hot Button areas.

How will you avoid answering intrusive questions?

CHAPTER 5:
KEEP ON PUSHING BUTTONS (PART 1)

The fourth method of D.A.R.K. is *Keep on Pushing Buttons.*

The Manipulator will keep on pushing your buttons from different directions: e-mail, direct mail advertising, a phone call about some special deal, saying "hi" to you at a networking event …. It goes on, and it doesn't stop.

How to Protect Yourself from a "Manipulator Who Keeps Pushing Your Buttons"

Know your vulnerable points, which we identified as your Desperate Hot Buttons. For example, I know people who use Amazon.com for retail entertainment: Oh, look what they're recommending to me!

If your credit card is overused, do not visit Amazon.com. Why? The Web site really exists for only one thing: to get you to buy stuff.

You need another kind of hobby.

I remember working one year for a major corporation. One afternoon, I felt lousy. I looked around, and I saw and heard people crunching potato chips and drinking Coke. The programmers were getting fatter—and the potato chip companies were getting richer. I didn't want to get heavier, so I didn't buy potato chips.

Instead, I typed "happiness" into a search engine. I was desperate. And what came up? You guessed it! A lot of products. During my next break, I went out and bought a book that had been brought to my attention.

The first powerful way we can protect ourselves is by taking a real look around. We seek to become present in the moment occurring now. We seek to become aware. Since we're talking about Amazon.com, let's look at a discussion about something researchers are calling Internet Addiction.

Columnist Gina Hughes, known as the Techie Diva, wrote the following:

"Here's a list of common symptoms [of Internet Addiction] to watch out for:

1. Lying about how much time is spent online.
2. General decrease of physical activity and social life.

3. Neglecting obligations at home, work, or school to spend time online.

4. Spending too much money on computer equipment or Internet activities.

5. Feeling a constant desire to be online when they're away from the computer.

6. Going online to escape real world problems.

7. Disregarding the emotional or physical consequences of being in front of a computer all day.

8. Denial of the problem."

The above information helps people become aware of a problem.

Our solution for vulnerability to a Manipulator who pushes our buttons is a three-fold process:

1) Become aware.

2) Identify how to become stronger.

3) Take action to improve your life.

First, to ensure that you are aware, return to your Desperate Hot Buttons listed in the previous chapter. In a moment, you will use your list to inspire your Counter-Actions. By writing a list of Counter-Actions, you will realize how to have an empowered response. When you use your Counter-Actions, you are taking action to improve your life.

Here are examples of Desperate Hot Buttons and appropriate Counter-Actions.

Desperate Hot Buttons

1. I'm fat.==> Counter-Action: I walk.

2. I'm lonely. ==> Counter-Action: I go to continuing education courses. I meet new people.

3. I need money. ==> Counter-Action: I am carefully researching options.

4. I'm 42 and I feel trapped. ==> Counter-Action: I now see

myself as an explorer. I am taking classes, reading books, talking with appropriate people to find new ways to express my natural brilliance.

About the Desperate Hot Button, "I'm fat": Fortunes have been made through late-night-TV infomercials that sell exercise equipment. As a Counter-Action, some of my clients tell themselves: "I don't need that new exercise equipment. In fact, I don't watch late night TV. I watch a DVD so no commercial can get at me when I'm vulnerable."

Now, it's your turn. Write a list in your personal journal of your Desperate Hot Buttons with an associated Counter-Action.

The next step is to put some Counter-Actions on your calendar. Go ahead! Pull out your day planner or PDA.

Remember the phrase: A goal is just a wish until you schedule it.

Point to Remember:
Manipulators keep pushing buttons.

Your Countermeasure:
Know your Desperate Hot Buttons and set up Counter-Actions. Then, be sure to take action using your strategic Counter-Actions.

How will you conceal your Desperate Hot Buttons and use strategic Counter-Actions?

CHAPTER 6:
KEEP ON PUSHING BUTTONS (PART 2)

Now, I'll share Part 2 about *Keep on Pushing Buttons*.

Many Manipulators have studied, rehearsed and

practiced techniques that work on other people. This leads us to:

Darkest Secret #4: Manipulators Use Your Subconscious Mind Against You

Manipulators use against you their knowledge of:
- Personality styles
- Neuro-Linguistic Programming
- Sales techniques and how to overcome objections

Study their examples on the next pages.

Manipulators study personality styles. They learn how to talk with you in ways that make you feel good, make sense, and make you feel that the Manipulator is just like you.

A Personality Style Technique

Talk in a manner that makes the person feel good.
Examples:
- A hard-charging Director likes to hear, "Good decision. The bottom-line is ..."
- A warm Relater likes to hear, "This is basically the same as what you have been doing. This will make things more comfortable for your team members ..."
- A precise Analytic likes to hear, "You can see for yourself with these graphs and tables ..."
- A flamboyant Socializer likes to hear, "Great idea! I'm sure your team will see how sharp you are for bringing this product into the process ..."

Countermeasure:

Read about personality styles. Identify what your personality style is. Then, get more information about the salesperson to verify his or her personality traits. If the deal is a big one, you may want to view his personal office space or even visit the person at home. Researcher John Gottman mentioned that you can learn much more about a person by seeing his or her personal space (room, office, etc.) than by listening to his public persona speech.

* * *

Manipulators study Neuro-Linguistic Programming. They learn how to guide you into a state of being that makes it easy to buy something.

Neuro-Linguistic Programming Technique of Mirroring-and-Matching

The person using this technique will change body posture to match yours. If you have your arms-folded, the person will (after about 20-30 seconds), fold his or her arms, too.

Countermeasure:

Smile. Because you now have added information. Don't say anything about the use of the technique to the person. If you catch someone doing Mirroring-and-Matching, you can slow the process down and remind yourself that this person is consciously trying to push your buttons.

* * *

Manipulators study sales techniques and how to overcome objections.

Sales Technique

Using questions to lead the prospective buyer. For example: "If we can get you the car in blue, you can own it today—right?"

Countermeasure:

Read about sales techniques. In the above question, we see four techniques.

1) The salesperson tries to pin you down with the idea that "blue" is the special detail that closes the sale.

2) Using the word "own" is more effective than saying "buy." People want to own things, but many are afraid to sign on the line and buy something.

3) "Own it today." Salespeople know that we are bombarded with an estimated 15,000 messages a day. The salesperson wants to place you in a good state of being for buying. And he or she wants to close the sale before you are distracted by something else.

4) Ending a question with "Right?" or "Don't you?" is a technique for gaining agreement.

When you recognize a sales technique, smile. Smiling puts you in a better mood. Researchers confirm that just putting a pen in a study-participant's mouth (which approximates a smile) can put the participant into a better mood. When you're in a better mood, you are stronger. Think of the old phrase, A technique known is a technique blown. When you know the technique, it loses power—and you get stronger.

The studies of personality styles, Neuro-Linguistic Programming and sales techniques, persuasion skills and negotiation skills are not bad in themselves.

But a Manipulator only cares about making the sale and has no concern about whether you get hurt in any way.

Manipulators know that people buy on emotion, and later justify with facts.

How do you know if something is a fact? Who told you? The salesperson? What is his or her agenda? Right! Make the sale!

How to Protect Yourself from "Manipulators Who Use Your Subconscious Mind Against You"

First, make efforts to know yourself better.

What Works on You?

For most parents, the safety of their children opens the door to the parents being vulnerable to manipulation.

A Manipulator uses ideas similar to these:

You need a new car. Why? Because you need side safety airbags. Oh, you have a son? Imagine your son is with you and BAM! A car crashes into the side of your car. Imagine being in the hospital and holding your son's hand as you pray that he will wake up from a coma.

The example above is "over the top." But have you noticed that some commercials show car crashes? Two people are driving along, having a fun time, when BAM! Their car is hit. The impact is so extreme that we feel that they must be severely injured. The next moment, we see them shaken but unhurt outside their smashed vehicle. My point: Manipulators prey on our fears.

What Makes You Vulnerable?
- Are you getting enough sleep? No? You're vulnerable.
- Are you eating nutritious foods or are you on a sugar-rush (or sugar-high)?
- Are you getting regular exercise?
- Are you getting rest and time away from work?
- Are you getting spiritually nourishing time on your spiritual path?
- Do you devote enough time with your family and friends?

To Protect Yourself from the Manipulation of Your Subconscious Mind, You Need a Good Ready Stance.

During the years I studied karate and other martial arts, I learned about a ready stance. In karate, I would stand in the cat stance. The front foot rests only on the toes, so if someone tries to sweep that foot, you won't fall down. You pull the front foot back and kick! For the sake of our discussion, I'm using the idea of the cat stance as an example of our Ready Stance.

What constitutes the Ready Stance that protects you from subconscious manipulation?

1) Enough sleep
2) Enough nutritious foods
3) Regular exercise
4) Enough rest and time away from work
5) Enough spiritually nourishing time on your spiritual path
6) Enough time with family and friends
7) Pattern-Interrupt Methods

When I mention Pattern-Interrupt Methods, I'm referring to techniques that enable you to disrupt trance-states.

Learn to Use Pattern-Interrupt Methods to Break the Trance Invoked by a Manipulator:

Top salespeople are trained to put you into a trance. Like a hypnotist, the top salesperson gets you into a state in which you easily say, "Yes. I'll buy it."

You need pre-need Pattern-Interrupt Methods. For example, I helped one of my clients install a Pattern-Interrupt method.

Joe knew that he was vulnerable to sales pitches. I had him close his right fist and tap it on the side of his chest and say fervently: "I am my own person! I am my own person!" This phrase became so thoroughly installed that he could break his trance (induced by a salesperson) by merely taping the side of his chest with his closed fist and hearing "I!" in his mind.

How to Counter the Urgency-Trance

Earlier, we talked about how a Manipulator uses methods to get us to feel urgent feelings. Oh, no! If I don't act now, I'll miss the sale (or the "limited-time, discount price").

Here's a personal example. In one year, I read 85 books. You can see that I am absolutely committed to learning, but this commitment also makes me vulnerable to someone's information-pitch that seems crucial to expanding my success.

I have my own Pattern-Interrupt Methods. I have certain thoughts that come up in my mind by reflex:

a) I can scope this guy out on the Internet.

b) I can read reviews of his book at Amazon.com.

c) I can read his book.

By simply thinking these thoughts, I drain the situation of urgent feelings. I can implement the above three steps. If the steps yield positive results, I can choose to invest money in the person's training program later.

Counter the Urgency-Trance when You Ask Questions and Give Yourself Permission "to Be Rude."

Years ago, a consultant tried to get me to hire his firm. I said, "I have to answer to the Board of Directors. I will need to ask you a few questions." In this way, I gave myself permission to ask any question—even questions that might seem rude—because I had to answer to a higher authority. If you don't have a Board of Directors to answer to, you can say the following:

- I need to talk this over with my husband/wife.
- I need to talk this over with my accountant.
- I'm sure my lawyer will have a number of questions.

The technique of saying that you must check in with someone else is an example of a *Pattern-Interrupt Method*. You interrupt the pattern that the salesperson uses to get you comfortable and in a buying mood. The salesperson wants to get you comfortable and then aims to pin you down so you admit that you have the sole authority to make a decision.

You break this pattern by replying with something like, "I need to talk this over with my accountant." If you watch closely, you might see the salesperson's face wince just a bit. You have just thrown the salesperson off his or her game.

Point to Remember:

Manipulators study personality styles, Neuro-Linguistic Programming, sales techniques, persuasion skills and negotiation methods.

Your Countermeasure:

Read about the Manipulator's tool kit (sales techniques, etc.). Develop a strong Ready Stance. Use a Pattern-Interrupt Method to break a trance. Also, do your homework before you go out to buy something: read consumers reports and talk to people who use the product you're considering.

How will you use a Pattern-Interrupt Method?

_____

_____

Summary of Strong Subconscious Methods

Book I included a number of Strong Subconscious Methods, revealed in the appropriate context. Next, note the list of various methods that we have discussed:

24 Methods to Protect Yourself
(Including Strong Subconscious Methods)

1. Breathe
2. Relax
3. Envision
4. Act on Aromas
5. Keep Moving
6. Smile

7. Identify the Crucial Detail
8. Use Questions to Deal With Feelings of Urgency
9. Use Questions that Help Your Intuition Speak Up
10. Identify Your Desperate Hot Buttons
11. Reframe Your Desperate Hot Buttons
12. Add Emotion and Take Powerful Action—Part One: Use Visualization
13. Use Lyrics and Music to Create Empowering Emotion
14. Use Movement to Create Empowering Emotion
15. Evasive Action: 8 Methods to Avoid Answering Questions (Designed to Reveal Desperate Hot Buttons)
16. 3-Step Process to Strengthen Yourself
a) Become aware.
b) Identify how to become stronger.
c) Take action to improve your life.
17. Use Counter-Actions Related to Desperate Hot Buttons
18. Counter a Personality Style Technique: Read about personality styles and identify your own personality style. Get more information to identify the salesperson's personality traits.
19. Counter a Neuro-Linguistic Programming Technique: Smile when you observe the Mirroring-and-Matching Technique.
20. Counter the Sales Technique that uses effective questions: Read about how salespeople use effective questions to guide you to buy today.
21. Stay strong with a good Ready Stance:
a) enough sleep, nutritious foods, exercise
b) enough rest and time away from work
c) enough spiritually nourishing time
d) enough time with your family and friends
22. Set up your own Pattern-Interrupt Methods

23. Counter the Urgency-Trance: have alternatives already in mind. (Examples: "I'll investigate this guy via the Internet; read reviews at Amazon.com; and read the person's book")

24. Counter the Urgency-Trance: Ask questions and give yourself "permission to be rude." (Say, "I'll have to take this to the Board of Directors" or "I need to run this by my accountant/attorney."

CHAPTER 7: HOW TEN BILLIONAIRES AND MILLIONAIRES PERSUADE OTHERS

This book is about turning the power to good. Positive persuasion methods of ten billionaires and millionaires are described below.

1. Bill Gates

Bill Gates emphasizes an intelligent approach to technical situations. He said, "The first rule of any technology used in a business is that automation applied to an efficient operation will magnify the efficiency. The second is that automation applied to an inefficient operation will magnify the inefficiency." He also said, "I think it's fair to say that personal computers have become the most empowering tool we've ever created. They're tools of communication, they're tools of creativity, and they can be shaped by their user."

2. Oprah Winfrey

Oprah Winfrey's television audience finds her persuasive because they can relate to her feelings. For example, she related her painful feelings in the August 2007 issue of *O, The Oprah Magazine*. Oprah mourned the death of her two-year-old golden retriever, Gracie. "Weeks have passed, and the pain has not subsided. Every time I think about it, my heart starts racing and I feel like I just got stabbed in the chest." Oprah wrote that she "got the message" to slow down and catch her breath when Gracie died. "I don't believe in accidents. I know for sure that everything in life happens to help us live."

3. Jack Canfield (co-creator of the *Chicken Soup for the Soul* series of books and numerous products)

Jack Canfield provides listeners with hope. He said, "Everything you want is out there, waiting for you to ask. Everything you want also wants you. But you have to take action to get it.... Most fears cannot withstand the test of careful scrutiny and analysis. When we expose our fears to the light of thoughtful examination, they usually just evaporate."

4. Mark Victor Hansen (co-creator of *the Chicken Soup for the Soul* series of books and numerous products)

Mark Victor Hansen's approach is to offer catchy phrases. His comments include: "Don't think it, ink it!" "When your self-worth goes up, your net worth goes up with it." "In imagination, there's no limitation."

5. Brian Tracy

Brian Tracy presents precise methods that are expressed simply and clearly. He wrote: "A major stimulant to creative thinking is focused questions. There is something about a well-worded question that often penetrates to the heart of the matter and triggers new ideas and insights." He said, "Successful people are always looking for opportunities to help others. Unsuccessful people are always asking, 'What's in it for me?'" And, "Goals allow you to control the direction of change in your favor." And finally, "Your decision to be, have and do something out of the ordinary entails facing difficulties that are out of the ordinary, as well. Sometimes your greatest asset is simply your ability to stay with it longer than anyone else."

6. Tony Robbins

Tony Robbins, in his presentations, energizes the listener.

He often has audience members clap their hands and exclaim, "Yes! Yes! Yes!" He delivers ideas that make intuitive sense. He said, "In life you need either inspiration or desperation." "My definition of success is to live your life in a way that causes you to feel a ton of pleasure and very little pain—and because of your lifestyle, have the people around you feel a lot more pleasure than they do pain." "One reason so few of us achieve what we truly want is that we never direct our focus; we never concentrate our power. Most people dabble their way through life, never deciding to master anything in particular." "Successful people ask better questions, and as a result, they get better answers." "The secret of success is learning how to use pain and pleasure instead of having pain and pleasure use you. If you do that, you're in control of your life. If you don't, life controls you." "The path to success is to take massive, determined action."

7. Warren Buffet (legendary investor and one of the wealthiest people in the world)

Warren Buffet is known for his plain speech. He said, "It's better to hang out with people better than you. Pick out associates whose behavior is better than yours, and you'll drift in that direction." And, "Only buy something that you'd be perfectly happy to hold if the market shut down for 10 years.... Your premium brand had better be delivering something special, or it's not going to get the business."

8. Richard Branson

Richard Branson is known for persuading the media to cover his adventurous stunts. Often he ties a stunt with one of his many companies. He said, "My vision for Virgin [companies] was ultimately summed up by Peter Gabriel, who once said to me, 'It's outrageous!' ... I rely far more on gut instinct than researching huge amounts of statistics. ... All the things that have happened to me, to the family and to

Virgin have taught me that you have to be prepared at all times to deal with surprises. You just develop a way of picking up your feet and getting on with it." And ...

"I had the ability to persuade them to say yes, and the obstinacy never to accept no for an answer."

9. Suze Orman (#1 *New York Times* best-selling author, known as "America's most trusted personal finance expert"):

Suze Orman is known for her straight-to-the-point comments: "In all realms of life, it takes courage to stretch your limits, express your power, and fulfill your potential.... It's no different in the financial realm." "A big part of financial freedom is having your heart and mind free from worry about the what-ifs of life." And finally, "People first, then money, then things."

10. Walt Disney

Walt Disney was a master storyteller. Walt Disney said, "I look for a story with heart. It should be a simple story with characters the audience really can care about. They've got to have a rooting interest." Walt persuaded his team members to improve each project. His term was in his comment: "We need you to plus this." He also said, "Give the public everything you can give them. Keep the place as clean as you can keep it. Keep it friendly." Finally, "The way to get started is to quit talking and begin doing."

From many of these effective people, we learn that speaking in a forthright manner gains attention.

CONCLUSION OF BOOK I

We've looked at the Darkest Secrets of Manipulators, and you are now armed with Countermeasures to protect yourself.

Now, I'm breathing easier. Writing this section of this book felt like running a sprint. My cautionary comments poured out of me.

Book II, which follows is about protecting yourself from the Darkest Secrets of Seduction Masters.

Let's move forward.

Which ideas from the above prosperous people capture your attention. How will you implement something similar in your own life?

BOOK II: DARKEST SECRETS OF SEDUCTION MASTERS—INTRODUCTION

Welcome to Book II. This is a special addition for this second edition. The previous version of this book focused only on persuasion. Some people mentioned to me that they needed help with situations in which they were particularly vulnerable—those in which they could be seduced.

Now, we cover the Seducer's methods with S.E.D.U.C.E.:

S — Select environments

E — Excite and promise

D — Dangle and snatch away

U — Use surprise and delight

C — Catch you in an emotional wave

E — Express

You can see that many of the moves that counter negative seduction are about making yourself a strong and happy person. (A negative seduction is a process in which a Seducer influences you to do things that, on reflection, you would feel bad about.)

Are You Vulnerable to Being Seduced?

Answer the following questions, and you'll discover your current state of strength or vulnerability:

1. Do you have hope?
2. Are you flowing forward such that you are growing and creating a better life?
3. Do you have fun every week?
4. If you're in a relationship, do you and your romantic partner regularly have intimate times together?
5. Did you do anything that you found fun and exciting in the last two months?
6. Do you have two friends or family members who really support you?
7. Do you have someone to confide in?
8. Are there regular situations in your life in which you feel competent and effective?

If you answered "no" to more than four of these questions, watch out!—you are vulnerable to being seduced. The good news is that this section of this book gives you the tools you need to become stronger.

Let's move on to the next chapter ...

CHAPTER 8: SELECT ENVIRONMENTS

(The first method of S.E.D.U.C.E.)

I was seduced in Disneyland!

Yes. By a park visitor who knew me.

My heart had been broken, and she (the Seducer) knew it. She also knew that Disneyland was a special place for me.

Sitting on the Splash Mountain ride with her snuggled in front of me, my emotions were hit by a tidal wave—and I don't mean just the Splash! of Splash Mountain.

Let's face it. There are reasons for a candlelit dinner, soft music, the dance floor, drinking champagne on a balcony with a view of the sunset—all this puts us in the mood.

These details stimulate us and move our emotions.

The Seducer carefully plans to place you in an environment that stimulates your senses. Suddenly, you are overcome with emotions that may have been lying dormant. If your self-esteem has recently taken a few hits, you may be vulnerable.

How to Protect Yourself from "Select Environments"

First, one master martial artist told me, "The best defense is not to be there." Married people are advised to avoid working late at the office with the hunk or beautiful fashion model. After a long, tough day at work, we're vulnerable. We're tired and we yearn for an escape. Often, the Seducer lies in wait just like a trap-door spider. Avoid being alone with a Seducer. One time, I was in a select audience, listening to best-selling author Zig Ziglar, who said, "When I'm on the road, I don't put myself in situations in which I'm alone with any woman.... I do not take my secretary out to lunch."

Second, if you are in a situation that changes into a negative seduction opportunity for the Seducer, you can still retain your power. Set up a Pre-need Pattern-Interrupt Method. Some of my clients close their fist, tap on their thigh and ask silently, "What is really going on here? Am I safe? Can I trust this person?" Also, some people ask, "Am I vulnerable now? Can I trust myself?"

Finally, be sure to avoid complaining to a Seducer about something that upsets you concerning your spouse (if you have one). It's amazing how the Seducer's comforting attention awakens our desires. If you need a comforting, sympathetic ear, see a counselor or get a dog!

Actually, having a dog or other pet is helpful because you receive unconditional affection. It is part of having a whole support system. We'll talk more about developing your support system as we continue to discuss how you can make yourself stronger.

Point to Remember:

The Seducer uses an environment to throw you off balance and give you an emotional rush.

Your Countermeasures:

Avoid being in a compromising situation. Don't work late with an attractive co-worker. Avoid discussing an argument between you and your spouse with a comforting Seducer. Use a Pattern-Interrupt Method, and use automatic questions like: "What is really going on here? Am I safe? Can I trust this person?" (Ask yourself, "Am I vulnerable now? Can I trust myself?")

How will you use a Pattern-Interrupt method to prevent negative seduction?

CHAPTER 9: EXCITE AND PROMISE

(The second method of S.E.D.U.C.E.)

Sarah would always remember this night. Charles arrived with a limousine and whisked her to the theatre for *Phantom of the Opera*. She loved the music, but she had never seen the musical on stage. Her heart pounded with excitement.

She could already picture it—her new life: this rich man whisking her to the theatre, soon the opera, then Cancun, Hawaii. Oh, the adventures they would have!

Oh yes! She would "give into the music of the night." He was so skillful. He played her like a violin.

"My God! Could this be the one?" she thought.

Later, her heart was torn to ribbons when he didn't return

her phone calls. Then he even changed his cell phone number. Cinderella bit the dust.

The Seducer Preys on Our Tendency to Form an Image of a Person

When I arrived at college the first year, I was hurting. I had left the city where I grew up, and I had just survived the breakup of my first love relationship (which had lasted two and a half years).

My desire for a connection led me to go on the "freshman retreat." That's when I met her. Susan was amazing. She was so giving and kind that she helped prepare the meals while the other freshmen relaxed and had fun. I was enraptured by this giving, spiritual, kind, young woman.

The truth (I later learned) was she was doing her job. Her job was to help prepare the meals. That was the deal that allowed her to attend this retreat.

While devoting time with her and becoming her friend, I learned that she was a kind person. But I also learned an important lesson. I had been in love with my image of who she was; rather, better wording is I had been infatuated with my image of who I imagined her to be.

I had made that image in my own mind. That image was based on my imagination.

* * *

An interviewer said, "That example was not about a Seducer toying with you. The image you had was your own fault."

Exactly!

This is my point. We need to remain aware of how our mind tends to work. At this moment, I am viewing the computer monitor and seeing the words as I type. But the truth is that my eyes are sensory receptors and my mind interprets what I see. Someone who reads a different language would see the words as gibberish. My point here is that my mind has been trained to see, perceive and interpret words. Through this book, your mind is being trained to be in the moment and stay aware so you eliminate vulnerability to negative seduction. The following countermoves can make you stronger and can actually enrich your life!

How to Protect Yourself from "Excite and Promise"

The solution is to make your life exciting and fulfilling. There is no shortcut. If your life is boring, you are vulnerable!

Life shrinks or expands in proportion to one's courage.
— *Anais Nin*
Just tell the truth. It'll save you every time. — Oprah Winfrey
So let's tell the truth.

Is your life exciting and fulfilling?

Take a moment. Writing your truthful answer in a journal would help you.

At this moment, my response is that I have been away from music for a while. Years ago, I was the lead singer and keyboard player for a band. More recently, I have written music that appears in my feature films and on my empowering audio programs. But now, I feel that I have been away from music too long.

Did you notice that? I started with "away from music for a while" and then I just switched to "I have been away from music too long."

This is the process of telling the truth to ourselves.... I just took this truthful response and set up an electronic piano so I can play from this moment forward on a daily basis.

In the next 20 seconds, in your personal journal, write five quick answers to this question: What would make your life exciting?

Adele, one of my clients said, "Oh, I guess going to

Cancun would be exciting."

I replied, "And ...?"

"Well, if I were acting in feature films, that would be better, I guess," she continued. Further into our discussion, I helped Adele realize that she could start to make progress towards acting in feature films by providing her headshot (photograph) to students at the local film school. She could hire a student to make a short film with her in it. This film, if it turned out well enough, could be part of her demo reel.

The point is that we can take small steps. Even small steps can bring excitement to our daily lives. For more strategies about this process, please see my book *Emotion-Motion Life Hacks*.

Now, let's look at the truth that's revealed in your answers to the next question:

What would create fulfillment in your life? (Write your answers in your personal journal.)

The Seducer knows that many of us are too busy and feel emptiness that's related to excitement and fulfillment.

The real defense against a Seducer is to have a fulfilling life. An important distinction is made by focusing on what really fulfills your heart. Author Judith Wright noted, "Fulfilling a hunger (craving of the soul) leads to a deep sense of satisfaction, while fulfilling a want leads to more wanting."

This is an important distinction. Adele wants excitement, and on the surface, she thought that going to Cancun would be the answer. But when I pressed her a bit, she realized that her hunger or the craving of her soul is to perform. That relates to her deep, heartfelt hungers to be seen, to be creative, to contribute to the joy of the audience, and more.

Author Judith Wright drew up a list of Spiritual Hungers:

"I hunger ...

To exist	To be seen
To be heard	To be touched
To be loved	To be affirmed
To express	To experience fully
To learn	To grow
To trust	To develop
To be known	To matter

To know another human being
To be close   To feel connected
To be intimate To love
To do what I came here on earth to do
To make a difference
To please God   To fulfill my purpose
To unfold my destiny
To feel connected to the greater whole
To be one with all
To know God"

When your life is filled with experiences that address the above Spiritual Hungers, you are inevitably stronger. You can resist a negative seduction. As I mentioned, a negative seduction is a process in which a Seducer is influencing you to do things that, on reflection, you would feel bad about.

The point is that a living, loving and growing human being avoids being on the edge of desperation.

When you feel desperate for excitement and fulfillment, you are vulnerable to your imagination making false images.

Here is the Countermeasure: use a Pattern-Interrupt. For example, my client Stephen taps the knuckles of his right hand with his fingers of his left hand. While making this physical movement, he asks himself, "Who is this person? Am I making this up? What are the facts? Where can I get more evidence?"

You will get more benefit from this book when you

identify where you are vulnerable and customize a way to use a Pattern-Interrupt.

Point to Remember:

The Seducer does things to get you excited. You can succumb to the promise of more and more excitement, fun and thrills.

Your Countermeasures:

Make your own life exciting and fulfilling. Set a Pattern-Interrupt so you can identify whether your imagination is creating a false image. If you have a spouse or partner, talk about what kind of exciting life the two of you want and how you could work on it together. Make your relationship lively.

How will you use an Pattern-Interrupt to double-check if your imagination is creating a false image?

CHAPTER 10: DANGLE AND SNATCH AWAY

(The third method of S.E.D.U.C.E.)

Have you ever had a long-distance relationship? So many of us feel like we're in heaven for the few hours or days in which we're with our loved one. These times are intense, exciting, romantic, and joyful!

They are followed by intense, longing-filled phone calls during the "desert-time" between the weekends together.

A vicious cycle is set up:

1. Pleasure
2. Pain of loss upon separating for a time
3. Longing to be with each other
4. Fear that somehow the last get-together was truly the

final experience of joy and love with this person

The Seducer plays this game—and worse!

The whole idea is that the Seducer dangles pleasure and then snatches it away.

The Seducer gets a person to fantasize about how good the next encounter will be.

A Seducer may say, "Next time we're together, I want to do _____ to you and you'll feel _____." (Fill the blanks with your favorite sexual fantasy.)

One important detail: the Seducer makes the encounters have short durations. It is easier to portray the perfect lover in a short time period. The Seducer has valid-sounding reasons about how he or she must go away on business or for something else.

You become the puppet on a string.

For example, my client Jonathan, who was in a long-term relationship, found himself drawn to Mindy, a co-worker. At one point, Jonathan saw Mindy hugging her male friend. Jonathan suddenly felt jealous. He told me, "I don't know where that jealous feeling came from. Mindy and I were not a couple!" The short story is that Jonathan left his partner for Mindy. We learn from this example that a Seducer does things to get a person to feel powerful emotions like jealousy and fear of loss.

How to Protect Yourself from "Dangle and Snatch Away"

We all need to acknowledge that we are vulnerable to feeling pain and longing.

In our lover, we seek and desire that which we do not have.
—Socrates

As I have mentioned earlier, our strong defense against a Seducer is already to have our life exciting and fulfilling. The idea is to minimize "that which we do not have"; then the

Seducer has less leverage over us.

Certainly, when one is single, one can naturally long for romantic love and closeness. However, we can experience other forms of love that fill us up in spiritual and psychological ways. Be sure to nurture your other relationships with friends and family. If you feel the need for support, you might find working with a counselor or therapist helpful.

It is the time to dare and endure. — Winston Churchill

The truth is that our interpretation of events is more powerful than the events themselves. When your life is full and you create your own happiness every day, you have a strength that makes you resistant to negative seduction.

Everything can be taken from a man or a woman but one thing: the last of human freedoms to choose one's attitude in any given set of circumstances, to choose one's own way. —Viktor E. Frankl

Some readers read these words and think, "Nice words but my feelings are what get me into trouble." Yes, I hear you!

This is the reason that we need to engage your emotions by setting up Pre-Need Pattern-Interrupts.

In his bestselling book *Blink*, Malcolm Gladwell points out that we can have an intellectual idea, but our subconscious conditioning can override our rational thought. Again, this guides us to focus on Pre-Need Pattern-Interrupts.

I have mentioned the process of a Pattern-Interrupt earlier, and now I will provide more information. The Pattern-Interrupt includes four components:

Pattern-Interrupt:
1. Choose physical component
2. Switch your thoughts
3. Gain awareness
4. Escape hatch

If you're hurting so much that you can't think straight, that is a Red-Alert Warning! It's time to set up a Pattern-Interrupt.

For example, my client Marina chose as her physical component tapping her right forefinger to the pad of her right thumb. It almost looks like the "okay" gesture. She needs to switch her thoughts. She uses the Switch Phrase, "What am I feeling?"

Here is how the process goes.

1. Marina feels upset because she is away from her boyfriend, Joseph.
2. She uses the "finger-thumb tapping" physical component.
3. She asks herself, "What am I feeling?"
4. "Lonely," her mind responds.
5. Now Marina is aware, and she uses her second Switch Phrase: "What do I want?"
6. "To feel love," her mind responds.
7. Now, Marina can use her escape hatch. She has a written list of how she can feel support.

Marina's Pre-written List of Support

1. Call my best friend Serena.
2. Deep breathe and say a prayer.
3. Write in my journal to let the feelings out.
4. Listen to soothing music.
5. Take a hot bath.
6. Take a walk.
7. Get into nature.
8. Listen to an encouraging audio program.
9. Other options.

The point is that Marina is skilled in working with her feelings of loneliness.

The more skillfully we take care of our personal feelings,

the less power a Seducer can have over us.

Point to Remember:

The Seducer keeps you off balance and dependent by dangling time together and then pulling the rug out from under you.

Your Countermeasure:

Set up a Pattern-Interrupt that includes a Pre-written List of Supports.

How will you implement a Pre-written List of Supports?

CHAPTER 11: USE SURPRISE AND DELIGHT

(The fourth method of S.E.D.U.C.E.)

Do you remember hearing a friend or yourself saying, "Oh! I'm so in love!" What a delightful feeling!

The Seducer knows the power of surprising the targeted person with gifts and unusual experiences. The Seducer preplans ways to get the person to experience a rush of delighted emotion.

If you're not experiencing delight on a regular basis, you are vulnerable when the Seducer uses pre-planned and well-orchestrated techniques to awaken your senses. Some Seducers can get you to ride a horse at sunset; to drink champagne on a tour boat on the San Francisco Bay; or to vacation in Hawaii.

Why Are Marriages So Vulnerable?

In a few words: a person falls in love because she likes how she feels about herself while she's with her loved one. She enjoys feeling special and cherished.

A man enjoys feeling admired and like a hero.

What happens after several years in a marriage? The parties take each other for granted and the emotion-deadening strain of routine sets in.

It gets even worse. Some married people form a neural association of their partner's face with disapproval and disappointment. To put it bluntly, according to researchers, a significant number of married women are intensely disappointed. And their disappointment shows in their faces and in the tone of their voice.

The husband feels like he's losing and can never win, which is devastating for the male ego. Boys and men have been conditioned to perform and achieve. A man wants to achieve for his beloved wife, so he feels like an utter failure.

It's just as difficult for women. According to researchers, women often feel terrible. They feel taken for granted. On a subconscious level, some feel, "If I were attractive enough, he would treat me as special. I so want to feel special."

Also, women feel unappreciated for all the work they do inside and outside the home.

What's the solution? How can we strengthen marriage so it is not so vulnerable to Seducers?

We must approach marriage as if it were a sacred and valuable job. What? Yes! If you suddenly earned a promotion, you would likely study and perhaps take classes so that you could achieve in your new position. The same dedication and openness to learning is needed in marriage. I invite you to read my book, *10 Seconds to Wealth: Master the Moment Using Your Divine Gifts*, so that you become acquainted with techniques to open the floodgates of romance and wealth in your relationship.

We can start from a premise emphasized by Dr. John Gray, author of *Men Are From Mars, Women Are From Venus*.

Dr. Gray says, "Men want a woman with a smile. Women want a man with a plan."

In a few words, this means that men want someone who will be pleased with their efforts, and women want a man to treat them as special; that is, she is so special that she deserves his efforts to form and then implement a loving plan.

Making a marriage strong requires significant effort.

For example, some years ago, my sweetheart set up a special event to take place during my birthday party. She prearranged with the guests that they would buy my new (at that time) book, instead of getting a potted plant or something else for me. We took a photo with everyone holding up copies of my book. Tears came to my eyes. One of my friends said, "Take it in, Tom. Take it in." You see, I was surprised by the wave of emotion that came over me. I write books because I truly want to serve the readers. I want to make a positive difference through my efforts. Here were my friends, expressing their solidarity with me; and I imagined a number of them reading my book and how I would be serving them.

This memorable moment was orchestrated by my loving sweetheart. To me, she is a hero!

Similarly, I know my sweetheart and her love of funnel cake. So I have arranged multiple vacations in Walt Disney World, where she gets funnel cake and the ambience of a refreshing theme park. I arranged funnel cake for her at the Santa Monica Pier in California.

We cherish each other and make significant efforts so that we feel loved.

The point is that a loving couple daily builds their connection and immunizes themselves from the approach of a Seducer.

How to Protect Yourself from "Surprise and Delight"

Simply put, you must arrange your own monthly "delight times."

My clients have noted these things that delight them:

1) the first moments when settling into a hot bath
2) dancing
3) singing
4) laughing with a group of friends
5) painting a picture
6) writing a poem
7) that winded but happy feeling after running or bicycling

The age-old advice, "know thyself," is especially valuable here.

Now, your personal journal write down your own list of Five Things that Delight Me.

Beware of How Easy It Is to Fall into Numbing Activities

People who habitually do activities that numb them are vulnerable to seduction. Why? Because numbing does not equal delight, and our heart hungers for delight.

My clients have noted these actions which, upon reflection, comprise merely numbing activities:

1) emotional eating
2) watching too much TV
3) shopping too much

Certainly, in moderation, any of these activities can be fine. But take care when you see that you reach for something numbing when you feel some form of discomfort. This reminds me of the phrase, "When the going gets tough, the tough go shopping!"

How can we identify numbing activities? Note how you feel after you do a habitual activity. Do you feel refreshed, excited and good about yourself? Or do you feel a twinge of shame or personal disappointment? This is the clue that the habitual activity is likely a numbing activity.

When you notice a numbing activity, stop, pull out your journal and ask yourself: Am I really feeling the effects of spiritual hunger? In the chapter *Excite and Promise*, I shared with you a list of spiritual hungers (such as, To Grow), as noted by author Judith Wright.

Please go back and review them. If you find that journal-writing is not attractive, you can talk with a close friend; or talk into an audio recording device and then listen to your own comments.

To really bring delight into your life and help you feel stronger, observe your habitual ways of talking.

Do you talk a lot about feeling overwhelmed, out of time, always working, doing more work than your partner does, or always putting someone else first? Realize that these feelings create vulnerability to seduction.

Instead, my clients have learned to focus on these ways of talking:

1) I'm looking forward to ...
2) Something that went well today was ...
3) I'm proud of myself for ...
4) I felt great when ...
5) Here's some good news ...
6) I felt really loved when ...
7) I felt a connection with God (Higher Power) when ...
8) I know I'm making a contribution (helping others) when I ...

Find ways to bring healthy, empowering actions into your daily routines.

Success on any major scale requires you to accept responsibility... In the final analysis, the one quality that all

successful people have ... is the ability to take on responsibility.
—Michael Korda

From the above quote, we are reminded to take responsibility for feeding our own inner child. The inner child is that part of you that feels vulnerable—and also, wants to experience fun.

Those who rely on excitement from the outside (such as from a Seducer) allow themselves to be needlessly vulnerable. But this is not for you. You, from this moment forward, can take responsibility for creating delight in your own life.

How Do You Surprise Yourself?

How can you arrange a surprise for yourself? Put yourself in situations in which energizing things may happen.

For example, over the years, I have discovered that I am energized when I attend a presentation by an author. Many positive things can happen. I may receive life-enhancing coaching when I ask the author specific questions; this has happened a number times. Often, having heard me speak up during the periods scheduled for audience interaction, another attendee starts a delightful conversation with me.

For me, it's delightful to be in a place (an author's presentation) where I can connect with other growth-focused people.

My point is that I do not know exactly how such an event will turn out. But I realize that the author's presentation is an event bursting with positive potential for joyful encounters and interactions.

So get out there. If you have an interest in tap dancing, aikido or hiking with a group, look for ways to join others who share similar interests.

You won't know if you have a found a life-giving hobby until you step outside your routine and your comfort zone.

Author Tony Robbins said, "Life is not boring. You are boring."

From this moment, you can expand your horizons.

Usually we think that brave people have no fear.
The truth is they are intimate with fear. —Pema Chodron

Point to Remember:

The Seducer orchestrates experiences in which the targeted person is overwhelmed by surprising feelings of delight.

Your Countermeasures:

Develop your sense of delight in daily life. Add life-giving hobbies and activities. Explore three positive activities over the next two weeks.

How will you add delight to your daily life?

CHAPTER 12: CATCH YOU IN AN EMOTIONAL WAVE

(The fifth method of S.E.D.U.C.E.)

When was the last time you were caught "in a wave of emotion?"

Does a memory leap to your mind?

No?

Uh-oh! You may be vulnerable to seduction. Why? Because people enjoy feeling an emotional release.

Some of my favorite feature films in my DVD collection are those that brought tears to my eyes, like *Field of Dreams, My Life* and *Bicentennial Man.*

One author said, "People are emotion-junkies."

The Seducer knows that people want to be with someone

who makes them feel better about themselves.

I remember the lyrics in a Beach Boys song: "Catch a wave; you'll be sitting on top of the world."

The concern is that if you don't experience an emotional release in a healthy way, at least a couple of times a month, then you may fall hard for a Seducer.

Many of us spend most of our time stuck in our head. That is, we focus on logic and on being effective and in control in the workplace.

Some of us hide from our deep longings.

Some of my clients have reported that they would enjoy letting go or surrendering to the passion of the moment. If a Seducer expresses compliments, appreciation or encouragement, the targeted person feels affirmed. The targeted person may suddenly feel good—perhaps, in a way that he or she has never felt before.

For example, a female Seducer knows that a man wants to feel strong and capable. My client, Stewart, reported that one woman told him during sex, "Oh! I think you found my G-spot!" He said that moved his feelings. He said, "That was the first time in my life that I felt good at sex." Stewart was longing to feel capable and "manly." At that point, he was vulnerable and willing to do just about anything for this Seducer.

My client, Millie, is missing something she doesn't often think about. When they were courting, years ago, she and her husband George went dancing. George is a clumsy dancer; he hates to dance. But when they were dating, he would do anything to win her heart. George and Millie are sitting on a powder keg. An explosion is imminent.

Just let Millie dance with Hank (the hunk at the office) during an office party, and she will be sideswiped with emotion.

If George wises up, he will invite Millie to take a ballroom dancing class with him each week. Then their relationship will be inoculated from the advance of Hank the hunk.

My point is that the Seducer is an expert at getting a person to feel big feelings—the feelings that sweep us off our feet, like a wave, and into the Seducer's bed.

We've heard of so many middle-aged people falling for a "hot, young thing."

What's going on there?

I mentioned earlier that Dr. John Gray, author of *Men Are from Mars, Women Are from Venus*, says, "Women want a man with a plan. Men want a woman with a smile." In a few words, that means women want a man to "treat them special." "Special" includes whisking them away on a night during which she doesn't have to plan anything.

Men want a woman with smile—a woman who admires them. The woman shows with her smile and expresses with her warm tonality: "Yes. You're doing well. I'm pleased. I'm satisfied. You're winning."

Sometimes, in life the solution is simple—not easy—but simple. If a woman says, "I'm so exhausted. I don't know how to feel satisfied!" The answer is: Learn! Make space. Get personal counseling.

My client, Matthew, still feels sadness about the end of a relationship over 10 years ago. He realizes now that he ran from a good woman because she was angry about some things: her being abused when she was a child, her job and Matthew. Matthew now says, "I think I ran away from her anger."

If you're in a relationship and you two are not experiencing positive feelings, it is often advisable that you run—not walk—to get some counseling.

In my book, *10 Seconds to Wealth*, I introduced the list of

"25 Things You Can Do to Help Me Feel Loved." For those in a relationship, it helps for both partners to write down and later share these lists.

The Seducer who catches an unsuspecting person in a wave of emotion inspires that person to say things like:
- "Oh! It was so much fun!"
- "Wow! I feel so alive."

I don't believe people are looking for the meaning of life as much as they are looking for the experience of being alive.
—*Joseph Campbell*

Being alive means different things to different people. To help yourself become stronger, open your personal journal and answer this question: What makes me feel alive?

We want to feel alive!

Years ago, I was dating a young woman who looked like a fashion model. At the time, I felt that I was dating "out of my league." She was thin and petite. We attended a music performance that didn't have enough seats for everyone. She sat on my lap for the whole performance. I was surprised by a wave of emotion. I felt like the Incredible Hulk—strong, powerful and big. My previous partners had all been about my height. This was a new, delightful feeling for me.

How to Protect Yourself from the Seducer Who "Catches You in a Wave of Emotion"

The solution is to devote significant attention, time and even money to create life-giving, positive emotion in your life.

One can never consent to creep when one feels an impulse to soar. —*Helen Keller*

Take control of your consistent emotions and begin to consciously and deliberately reshape your daily experience of life.
—*Tony Robbins*

The idea is to identify what truly moves your emotions.

Write a list in your personal journal that answers this question: What truly moves your emotions?

Now, identify positive, healthy ways that you can experience energizing emotions. You can make plans to:

a) enjoy laughter with friends

b) experience support from family members or a counselor

c) enjoy the wonder of trying something new, perhaps by taking a class

Write a list in your personal journal that answers this question: What positive ways can you find to experience healthy emotions?

Be Wary of How You Can Fall for Someone Who Is Charismatic.

The American Heritage Dictionary defines charisma as "personal magnetism or charm."

WordNet defines charisma as "a personal attractiveness or interestingness that enables you to influence others."

Author Roger Dawson identified these *12 rules for projecting charisma:*

1. Treat everyone you meet as if he or she is the most important person you'll meet that day.

2. Develop a sensational handshake.

3. Notice the color of their eyes as you shake hands.

4. As you shake hands, put out a positive thought.

5. Give sincere compliments.

6. Catch people doing something right.

7. Looks do matter! [The important thing is to do a lot with what you've been given.]

8. Smile for the magic two seconds longer than they do.

9. Take a check-up from the neck down. [Keep your clothes pressed and attractive.]

10. Push out empathy.

11. Respond to people's emotions, not to what they say.

12. Maintain a childlike fascination for the world in which you live.

Now, that you are aware of these tactics, you can be observant. If you find that someone is doing one of these actions and the situation feels forced, you can slow things down so you have time to reflect.

You can also use a Pattern-Interrupt. My client Kasandra taps her thumb and forefinger while repeating these questions in her head: "What's really happening here? Am I safe? Is this person genuine?"

In this way, Kasandra has a quick, easy and pre-programmed way to wake herself up from the daze created by a Seducer. Her Pattern-Interrupt is as effective as the ring of an alarm clock.

Before a negative-seduction situation, you need to practice your Pattern-Interrupt. Tony Robbins pointed out that pianos go out of tune, and it is only natural to tune the piano repeatedly over the years. I am recommending the same process for keeping you strong. Keep practicing your Pattern-Interrupt Method.

Point to Remember:

The Seducer orchestrates experiences so that you are caught in an emotional wave.

Your Countermeasure:

Use a Pattern-Interrupt Method to wake yourself up!

How will you set your own Pattern-Interrupt Method?

CHAPTER 13: EXPRESS

(The sixth method of S.E.D.U.C.E.)

What makes a Seducer dangerous? The Seducer expresses in ways that connect with your inner longings—longings that you may not even know you have!

For example, a number of middle-aged executives have affairs with their executive assistant. An executive assistant can soothe his or her boss' ego by:

a) providing support and devotion to the boss' goals

b) providing verbal appreciation: "You're so good at that."

The Seducer knows how to selectively praise the person.

Psychologists studying behavior have noted that one can get a pigeon pecking at a bar all day long. One starts by rewarding the pigeon for being anywhere near the bar. Soon the rewards require movements that come close to pecking the bar. Finally, the pigeon is rewarded for pecking the bar.

Often, I mention to my audiences:

"A man is like a pigeon. Reward him if he's anywhere near what you want him to do."

The Seducer knows this process.

As we noted earlier, men want to feel strong and capable. And women want to feel special and cherished.

Take out your journal and write the answer to this question: What would someone need to say or do to get you to feel special?

Are you now getting what you need to feel special?

If not, you're vulnerable to seduction!

And let's face it—you're probably not having enough fun in your life.

But, wait a minute! What if you do not have a romantic partner at this moment?

Who can cherish you?

You.

"Yeah, right," some readers respond.

Think about it. Who knows you best?

That is a trick question.

Some of us have devoted years to being "a good parent, a good co-worker, a good friend." Along the way, we shut down emotionally.

How are you nurtured? How do you practice extreme self-care?

The Seducer knows that many people are terrible at taking care of themselves.

How to Protect Yourself from the Seducer Who "Expresses Admiration, Nurturing, and More"

Get some nurturing now! I mean it.

Write your answers in your personal journal to this question: *10 Ways I Can Nurture Myself Today.*

It is helpful to have items on your list that do not depend on anyone else participating. You can choose to take a hot bath, read an enjoyable book, go for a walk, meditate, pray or write in your journal.

You can include other ideas that involve friends: make a telephone call to a friend, take a walk with friend or meet for tea or coffee.

Try new, appropriate things to increase your feelings of being nurtured.

Take the first step in faith. You don't have to see the whole staircase, just take the first step. — Martin Luther King, Jr.

For a married couple, it is important that both partners stretch and put effort into helping the other person feel nurtured. For example, a man who is a "strong, silent type" and who does not stretch to express his loving care for his mate can find himself strong, silent—and alone.

We all need to learn to express loving feelings and

supportive gestures to help one another.

The Idea, Express, Has Different Facets.

When we look at the elements of expression we find that:

1. The Seducer expresses what we want to hear, see and feel.

2. In the Seducer's presence, we express a part of ourselves that may have been suppressed or undiscovered.

3. Subconsciously, we express to ourselves, "I feel better about me when I'm with this person [the Seducer]."

Element #1: The Seducer Expresses What We Want to Hear, See and Feel.

A number of men prove vulnerable to the attentions of a younger woman. How? She can verbally express, "Oh, you're so good at that." That is, she expresses admiration. The vulnerable man enjoys seeing the look of admiration on her face. And the younger woman may put her hand on the man's arm in a way that conveys, "You are special. You're so manly and attractive. I want you."

Sometimes, a friendship becomes romantic when a woman is crying and the man takes her in his arms and comforts her. He feels strong and capable. Some Seducers are terrific actors, and they can convey the emotion that reels us in.

Some Seducers say all the words we have been longing to hear for years. Imagine what you'd like to hear. Would you like to hear: "Oh, you're really sexy," or "Oh, you're such a good person and you're so smart …"?

The point is to know yourself so that you realize what you're longing for. Then, you can remind yourself to go slowly if you have even a vague feeling that the person is not genuine.

Element #2: In the Seducer's Presence, We Express Part of Ourselves That May Have Been Suppressed or

Undiscovered.

Nancy simply gushes as she tells her friend Maybelle, "Oh! I never thought I could do that. But when Steve took me skydiving, I was surprised that I ..."

Part of the Seducer's bag of tricks is to take the person someplace where he or she will feel a rush of adrenaline. As I mentioned, it worked on me at Splash Mountain.

Petrina seduced Matthew in her home recording studio. She taught him to play a few notes on an electronic piano while she recorded a song with him. Matthew felt the rush of succeeding at something he had never done before.

If the Seducer gets the intended target to do something that inspires personal feelings of courage and strength, the Seducer is halfway home. When we feel strong, we like ourselves better—and this positive experience colors our impression of the Seducer.

An interviewer said, "It sounds like all seduction is negative. I mean, it's good when a new person helps you experience something new in life like traveling, self-defense, filmmaking, public speaking, gourmet cooking ... This is what makes a new person attractive to us."

"Exactly!" I replied. "This how we make new friends and have a varied and fulfilling life. But the big question is, what is the new person's intention? Dating is about exploring and getting to know someone. Let's remember that negative seduction is about doing something that may leave us with regrets. Our goal here is to be aware of our environment, the new person and the situation. We want to be able to make good personal choices."

I continued, "Researchers have found that if you get someone [the test-subject] excited, the person will think that someone nearby is exciting."

"Again, our goal is to be aware of the whole situation. It

takes time to see if a new person is genuine or not. It takes a lot of energy to be phony, and a Seducer can falter and be seen for what he or she really is," I concluded.

Element #3: Subconsciously, We Express to Ourselves, "I Feel Better About Me When I'm with This Person [the Seducer].

Let's face it. We approach a relationship because we want to feel better, happier and more fulfilled. It comes down to being with someone who makes us feel better about ourselves. Many Seducers get their targeted people to feel, "I'm really okay. This admirable person likes me/loves me."

The strong, negative seduction-resistant person takes action to fill his or her fuel tanks.

Here are fuel tanks:

1) I feel good about myself.
2) I feel admired.
3) I feel like I'm special.
4) Someone will support me/protect me/watch out for me.

1) I feel good about myself.

You can make progress with this. It will take some work. Some of us do well by getting a therapist and/or a coach. We learn to practice something called radical self-care. We learn to give ourselves credit for the good that we do. Some of us write in a journal each evening to pat ourselves on the back for every kind, courageous or helpful action we took during the day.

2) I feel admired.

Put yourself in situations in which you can excel. If you're a good cook, take a cooking class and explore new recipes. You will be in your element. The teacher or another student may say, "You're really good at this."

Develop your friendships. Be around people who are supportive and who express appreciation and admiration for your good points. Some people ask, "Where do I find people like that?" One answer is at workshops to help people develop loving ways of relating. These people are seeking to improve their skills in communicating.

3) I feel like I'm special.

Treat yourself like someone who is special. How would you show your best friend that you appreciate, admire and cherish him or her? What do you wish someone who loves you (or who could love you) would give you? How can you do that for yourself?

The point here is that many of us need to begin this way: Act as if you are ... then you become what you're aiming for. Imagine how you would act if you were as kind, courageous or helpful as you might become. Then reward yourself for any small step in the right direction.

4) Someone will support me/protect me/watch out for me.

How can you protect yourself in a healthy way? Which professionals might you hire to help you? Perhaps a personal trainer, a nutritionist or a personal coach. Some readers will immediately protest that they do not have the funds to hire help. I know of people who get therapy at a local university for psychology interns. These interns help clients while a licensed therapist supervises the process. The cost? $10 a session (in many locations).

Ask your friends for help. How? Sarah asks her friend: "Cindy, I have a question. I could use help with _____ and _____. Would you be comfortable in helping me with one of those two things?"

* * *

Life can be pulled by goals just as surely as it can be pushed by drives. – Viktor E. Frankl

When we are no longer able to change a situation—we are

challenged to change ourselves. – Viktor E. Frankl

As I noted earlier, often what we seek in another person is what we feel is lacking in ourselves.

The solution is for us to expand our horizons. One of the most important things for personal growth is whether we are coachable. That is, can we take in new ideas and adapt?

The test of a first-rate intelligence is the ability to hold two opposed ideas in mind at the same time and still retain the ability to function. – F. Scott Fitzgerald

So we can both be knowledgeable and also need new ideas and experiences. Some people hold a metaphor that life is a classroom. That metaphor can be empowering.

What do you want to learn? What can help you experience more fulfillment in life? Please note your answers in your personal journal. Then use your day planner and schedule activities for your personal enrichment. The person who lives a full life is strong and resilient.

In a nutshell, express your needs and find ways to fulfill them.

Write in your personal journal, the answers to these two questions.

a) In what ways do you feel vulnerable or inadequate?

b) How can you get training to become more effective in this area?

Place the answers to a) and b) immediately next to each other.

Point to Remember:

The Seducer expresses admiration and gets the targeted person to feel special.

Your Countermeasures:

Make plans and take action so that you are personally growing and adapting ... and feeling stronger and fulfilled. Also, make sure to devote time with supportive people who express appreciation for your efforts and good will.

CONCLUSION TO BOOK II

In Book II, we covered the Darkest Secrets of Seduction Masters:

S — Select environments
E — Excite and promise
D — Dangle and snatch away
U — Use surprise and delight
C — Catch you in an emotional wave
E — Express

We learned many countermeasures that reveal that becoming strong and happy is the true way to avoid falling for negative seduction.

In Book III, we will explore methods so that you make a great first impression. You will learn how to turn seduction-power to good.

Now, you'll open the door to more enjoyment.

BOOK III - MAKE A GREAT FIRST IMPRESSION & TURN SEDUCTION-POWER TO GOOD

Introduction

Imagine that you could truly turn persuasion and seduction secrets to good. What if you could make a great first impression?

What if you meet the perfect romantic partner and you want to make sure that you become a happy, long-term couple? In Book III, we will explore methods so you can make a terrific connection with a new person.

It is with relief that I return to my usual style of writing — positive and energizing.

To improve your personal dating process, you will learn to:

- eliminate the usual discomfort many of us feel in

social situations
- make a great first impression
- make a genuine and enjoyable connection with a new person
- express confidence
- identify what romance is to you and start experiencing more today!
- learn how to find your soul mate faster

To be persuasive and yes, even seductive, you need to express your True Self.

Your True Self is that part of you that is naturally brilliant and naturally courageous.

On the other hand, many of us spend much of our time in our Ego, also called The False Self. The False Self is made of fear. When we think and act from the Ego, we feel vulnerable and small. Many people express anger. Anger is fear, twisted.

However, you will learn to shift to your True Self.

When you express your True Self, your natural brilliance makes you attractive. People are attracted to aliveness.

Let's return to Joseph Campbell's comment: "I don't believe people are looking for the meaning of life as much as they are looking for the experience of being alive."

In a sense, people are attracted to those who express aliveness—as if their subconscious mind says, "Maybe your aliveness and sense of adventure will rub off on me."

Expressing aliveness is part of making a great first impression.

On a number of occasions, I've given the presentation, "First Impressions Are Everything: Breaking the Four-Second Barrier." The four-second barrier includes fifteen judgments a new person makes about you in just four seconds. It goes as fast as "Hi—2—3—4—Next!"

Along these lines, we notice the insights that Malcolm Gladwell wrote in his book, *Blink: The Power of Thinking Without Thinking*. He describes the Adaptive Unconscious which is the part of the brain that leaps to conclusions in those first precious seconds. He also notes that the Adaptive Unconscious makes quick judgments based on very little information. Making these quick judgments is something that Gladwell labels rapid cognition.

To make a great impression, we need to offer pleasing input to the Adaptive Unconscious. Then the new person's rapid cognition can be favorable to us.

Malcolm Gladwell wrote, "Perhaps the most common—and the most important—forms of rapid cognition are the judgments we make and the impressions we form of other people."

He continues:

"Our first impressions are generated by our experiences and our environment, which means that we can change our first impressions—we can alter the way we thin-slice—by changing the experiences that comprise those impressions. If you are a white person who would like to treat black people as equal in every way—who would like to have a set of associations with blacks that are as positive as those that you have with whites—it requires more than a simple commitment to equality. It requires that you change your life so that you are exposed to minorities on a regular basis and become comfortable with them and familiar with the best of their culture, so that when you want to meet, hire, date, or talk with a member of a minority, you aren't betrayed by your hesitations and discomfort …. [Our] unconscious attitudes may be utterly incompatible with our stated conscious values."

We can note that Gladwell proposes a noble plan to

change our environment to modify the Adaptive Unconscious's automatic judgments. But we also acknowledge that many individuals will, instead, continue to judge things automatically with their Adaptive Unconscious. These people will take their first impressions as truth. This means we need to cater to a new person's Adaptive Unconscious.

Gladwell gives us the clue to how we can cater to the Adaptive Unconscious. He writes, "If we can control the environment in which rapid cognition takes place, then we can control rapid cognition."

How do we control the environment and make a good first impression? We use the methods represented in the C.O.N.N.E.C.T. process.

I chose the word connect with care. The focus on making a great first impression often causes trouble and grief. Many of us feel shy or fearful because we are trying to "make something up" or "pretend." Gladwell talked about being "betrayed by your hesitations and discomfort." Hesitation and discomfort arise for many of us when we try to "pretend" we're someone special or attempt to pretend that we feel confident. This type of pretending has been part of the traditional paradigm of making a good impression.

Many of us who are trying to make a great first impression actually feel subconsciously defensive. That's why we must get away from the paradigm of making a great first impression in favor of making a great connection.

A key point is that if we make attempts to impress someone, we can often fail because we're attempting to sugarcoat the fear that is present with the Ego.

But when we shift to expressing our True Self and making a true connection, we are free of the Ego's paradigm.

This leads us to this insight:

A great first impression is a great connection.

How does one's spirit enter this discussion? It comes from identifying the difference between one's Adaptive Unconscious and one's intuition. Intuition comes from the True Self.

On the other hand, the Adaptive Unconscious often is formed by reactions to painful experiences during childhood. Thus, the Adaptive Unconscious is formed in a great measure by our Ego. As I mentioned earlier, the Ego is made of fear.

Your spirit and True Self relate to your intuition, which invites you to do things that will help you grow and expand the adventure, romance and joy in your life.

However, the Ego (with the quick judgments of the Adaptive Unconscious) will often get you to contract, to think, "This is good enough," and "Don't do that—you could get hurt."

We still need a new paradigm for making a good first impression. This better paradigm is to focus on making the great connection. Intuition is valuable in the connecting process. The focus on making a great connection eliminates fear. We step away from the Ego (fear) and toward the True Self. We put the other person at ease. We make the new person feel important. We create rapport. The Merriam-Webster's Medical Dictionary defines rapport as:

1) relation characterized by harmony, conformity, accord, or affinity [and]

2) confidence of a subject in the operator (as in hypnotism, psychotherapy, or mental testing) with willingness to cooperate.

Nothing gets done without rapport and agreement.

The good news is you will learn how to make a great first impression by creating rapport.

This material about making a great first impression relates directly to the subtitle of this book: *Turn the Power to Good*. While completing this book, my team members and I were clear that many readers would like to become persuasive and seductive. For this reason, we are directly addressing an essential part of persuasiveness: the ability to make a great first impression.

Avoid 7 Rapport-breakers and
Use Replacement Behaviors to Create Rapport

Many people who come home after a social event and say "That didn't go well" have unfortunately fallen prey to Rapport-breaking Behaviors.

Here are the 7 Rapport-breakers to avoid:

1. Talking too much about oneself
2. Using a fake smile
3. Hesitating (coming across as not confident and not having anything valuable to offer)
4. Dressing inappropriately
5. Lacking energy
6. Negative talking (complaining and poor me stories)
7. Failing to take leadership of the conversation

In order to accomplish permanent behavior change, we need to put in a replacement behavior for any behavior we want to eliminate. The C.O.N.N.E.C.T. methods are behaviors that will help you make a great first impression.

Remember: our real focus is making a great connection. When we talk about connection, we talk about bringing goodness and spirituality to all that we do. That is turning the power to good. Gandhi said, "Where love is, there God is also." We are not alone. Higher Power goes with us in our efforts to find somebody to love.

This is the C.O.N.N.E.C.T. process that we will use:

C — Come across with life

O — Open with a smile
N — Nurture positive stories
N — Notice what's working
E — Engage definite moves
C — Clothe yourself as a trusted advisor
T — Target listening-mode first

Just before we move on to the chapters that detail the C.O.N.N.E.C.T. methods, let's look at romance. If we want something in a vague way, we may not get it. We will likely be on a hit-and-miss journey. Therefore, get clear about what romance is to you and move toward experiencing more romance.

Let's Identify Romance and Look at Ways to Experience More of It

Dictionary.com includes the following in a definition of romance: "to court or woo romantically; treat with ardor or chivalrousness; to court the favor of or make overtures to; play up to."

Let's look at synonyms of romance: "story, fiction, allure, fascination, and exoticism."

The American Heritage Dictionary includes these words in a definition of romance:

- A love affair.
- Ardent emotional attachment or involvement between people; love.
- A strong, sometimes short-lived attachment, fascination, or enthusiasm for something.
- A mysterious or fascinating quality or appeal, as of something adventurous, heroic, or strangely beautiful.
- A long fictitious tale of heroes and extraordinary or mysterious events, usually set in a distant time or place.

- An artistic work, such as a novel, story, or film, that deals with sexual love, especially in an idealized form.

No wonder we want more romance! "I'll have two please!"

Many of us feel that romance is connected to true love. Maria Rodale, co-author of *It's My Pleasure*, wrote, "True love is when both people have room to grow and evolve together and enjoy the journey (not without its bumps and crying fits, however!). True love is when you find someone with whom you can be your true self."

Let's face it. Our True Self quietly whispers, I want to experience romance. The spiritual truth is that ultimately we influence how and when we experience romance. What? The point is that you need to make it okay for yourself to enjoy a daily amount of romantic elements in your life.

Remember the words in the definitions above: allure, fascination, exoticism; ardent emotional attachment; love; something adventurous, heroic, or strangely beautiful.

When you bring more life (and romance) to your life, you become attractive!

An interviewer asked, "What about married people? How can they experience reignited romance?"

Dr. Helen Fisher provided this answer: "How do you ignite mad romantic passion in another? Do novel things together."

There is no shortcut here. Loving spouses need to make plans and put money aside for doing novel things together.

Now, I invite you to do as homework novel things that you really enjoy in your daily life. Do you love flowers? Get some and place them in your living room. Do you love to laugh? Set your Digital Video Recorder (like a Tivo unit) to record funny shows. For example, I tend to watch something funny every day (even briefly). Thus, I make sure to enjoy laughter each day.

Write in your personal journal the answer to this question: In the past, what "romantic moments" have you enjoyed? Remember the words: allure, fascination, exoticism; ardent emotional attachment; love; something adventurous, heroic, or strangely beautiful.

Write in your personal journal the answer to this additional question: In the future what romantic moments would you like to enjoy? Again, remember the words: allure, fascination, exoticism; ardent emotional attachment; love; something adventurous, heroic, or strangely beautiful.

Special note: One of my friends has traveled all around the world—with women-friends, by herself, and with a male romantic partner (when in a relationship). Her life has a vast catalogue of romantic moments. She has managed to do this on various incomes. One time she owned a business. Later, her savings had dwindled, and she worked as an office assistant. At other times, she has worked as temporary catering team member (like a waitress). It's all about saving a portion of whatever income one has.

When our goals and dreams are clear, we get more personal energy. We then can make efforts to make dreams come true—including the dream of sharing your life with a terrific romantic partner. Now, in your personal journal write a list of what romantic moments you would like to share with a romantic partner. (Don't hold back! Watching the sunset in some exotic location, holding hands on a cruise boat to Alaska, snuggling in bed on a Sunday morning … Let your imagination fly free!)

Now, we're ready to learn how to make a great connection.

We know what we want.

Let's make it happen through the next sections of this book…

How will you connect to the essences of your goals and dreams?

CHAPTER 14:
COME ACROSS WITH LIFE
Book III—Part I
Make a Great First Impression
1. Come Across with Life
Overcome Rapport-breaker #1: Avoid Lacking Energy

Once again, we return to Joseph Campbell's words: "I don't believe people are looking for the meaning of life as much as they are looking for the experience of being alive."

The point is that people enjoy being around energy-creators. They like to avoid energy vampires. It is crucial that you do things in your life that fill you with enthusiasm. Do what you love, and you shine! If painting brightens your life, be sure to do it—even if you only have fifteen minutes to do so every other day. Be sure to devote time to being with people you care about. You are filled with life as you engage with life.

When I meet someone new, I ask a few questions and help the person recall a personal activity that inspires enthusiasm. I often ask, "What are you looking forward to?"

When you ask someone, "What are you looking forward to?" you need to be ready to give your own answer to the question. Your answer is an opportunity for you to shine and express your aliveness.

The point is that you need to know and practice expressing what in your life makes you feel joyful.

Some time earlier in my life, I wore a tie that had musical notes on it. Like a reflex, many people's reaction was, "That's a nice tie." If the energy of the conversation felt appropriate, I smiled and replied, "Oh, thanks. It inspires me, because sometimes I compose music." The new person responds, "You compose music?"

I smiled and replied, "Yes. For my feature films and audio programs..."

Then, I turned the conversation light back on the new person with a question such as, "How do you know our host, Sam?"

I did not launch into a monologue that includes items from my resume. My comment related to my tie is designed to "sprinkle" (like a condiment) a detail. Later on, the person can ask me a question about my filmmaking activities or audio programs.

Remember this powerful process of sprinkle a detail and then ask a question that returns the light of the conversation to the new person.

Be sure to have things in your life that you experience joy and enthusiasm about.

My audiences have mentioned the following:
- painting
- hiking
- dancing
- volunteering

Be sure to let your enthusiasm show in your smile and tone of voice.

Principle:
Come across with lively energy.
Power Question:

How can you focus on what makes you feel alive and vibrant?

CHAPTER 15: OPEN WITH A SMILE
2. Open with a Smile
Overcome Rapport-breaker #2: Avoid the Fake Smile

A smile makes any face attractive. As a feature film director, I have worked with a number of people I describe as "stereotypically attractive." Some people say that these individuals are "so good looking that they can be fashion models." We see that when the camera is off, their faces are often dark, tired and listless. On the other hand, a natural smile brightens any face.

The Genuine Smile rises and falls naturally.

When trying to make a great first impression, a number of people make a mistake by trying to paste a fake smile on their face. They would do better to have a genuine smile rise and fall naturally.

How do you express a genuine smile? Think thoughts that inspire a genuine smile.

For example, when I direct actors on the set of my motion pictures, I help them connect with two things:1) appropriate thoughts and 2) the objective.

When an actor (or someone wanting to make a great first impression) wants to smile sincerely, she needs to think appropriate thoughts. These thoughts are like a silent monologue that some actors write on their copy of a screenplay.

Here are examples of appropriate thoughts:
a. "Hi. You're going to be glad we connected."
b. "I'll be listening to you. You'll enjoy that."
c. "This is fun. Tonight, I'll meet new friends."
d. "It's fun to listen to other people. I just ask a few

questions, and the new person enjoys talking about herself."

Above I mentioned how actors focus on "the objective," such as, "I want to convince her that I care about her." When an actor is clear about her objective, she naturally and easily changes her behavior in an effective manner. Intuitively, she knows when to nod or smile.

For a first impression event, prepare by having a clear objective in mind. The form of the objective is, "I want to [verb] to [a person] so that person does [action]."

Here is a useful objective: "I want to put the new person at ease so she smiles and says she wants to stay in contact."

To create a genuine smile, you need to connect with your positive energy. It helps to memorize certain trigger words that release your positive energy.

Some of my clients use these phrases:

1) I ask a question. I listen. And we have fun together.
2) What a blessing! I'm doing good by listening.

In the previous chapter, I mentioned that we come across as being alive by preparing to talk (briefly) about what brings us joy in our daily life.

Some of my clients create opportunities to smile with these responses:

1) I'm looking forward to getting back to my painting tomorrow. I always feel good painting trees. (A natural smile crosses her face.)
2) Hi, I'm Sandy. And you are …? (A natural smile crosses her face because she likes her name. She changed it from "Sandra.")

One of my clients places a lavender-scented potpourri in her car so she enjoys her ride to a social event. Recalling the scent brings a natural smile to her face.

To wake up your spirit, be sure to add more things to your life that get you to smile: words, music, body posture (perhaps Tai Chi, Yoga, dancing or aerobics) and an aroma.

Principle:
Your face reveals your feelings; connect with your positive energy.

Power Question:
What makes you smile? What triggers can you set in place—words, music, body posture or aroma—so you can be energetic?

CHAPTER 16:
NURTURE POSITIVE STORIES AND OBSERVATIONS

3. Nurture Positive Stories and Observations

Overcome Rapport-breaker #3: Avoid Negative Talking—Complaining and Poor Me Stories

To make a great impression, you need to create rapport and guide the person you are with to have good feelings in your presence. Talk only about positive topics. As I mentioned earlier, ask, "What are you looking forward to?" Be prepared to respond with what you are looking forward to.

Before a networking event or social occasion, prepare by choosing the positive comments and anecdotes you will share. Avoid complaining and poor me stories.

To nurture positive stories and observations, you need to do your homework. You need to create a positive personal life. One great thing you can do is to set up a personal victory every morning. For example, most days, the first thing I do is write. No matter what else happens during the day, I have had a personal victory. I also set a goal that is doable for me—writing 500 words. On many days, I write in the morning and follow this with 30 minutes of exercise. I have already done things that I feel good about.

If someone asks me about my day, I might reply, "Things are going well. This morning I was writing and I had fun with an idea about ..." In this way, I talk about fun and ideas.

Some people paint in the morning or do some other self-nurturing activity.

Positive Observations Can Include Sincere Compliments.

I have a friend who gives sincere compliments:

a. "Oh, that tells me something about you. You're very detail-conscious."

b. "That's another example of why people trust you."

c. "Wow! You always come up with a creative solution that makes things work."

Make positive observations the way my friend does, and people will enjoy being in your presence.

Principle:

Express positive stories and comments, because this will make you attractive.

Power Question:

What positive things have you enjoyed in life? What personal victories can you create daily? Would you like to record these positive items in a daily gratitude journal?

CHAPTER 17: NOTICE WHAT'S WORKING

4. Notice What's Working

Overcome Rapport-breaker #4: Avoid Failing to Take the Lead in the Conversation

We can lead a conversation in two ways—by the questions we ask and the things that we respond to. The idea is to respond to positive details; that is, notice what's working. An experiment was conducted in which a class was able to get a teacher to stand in a certain place based on how well the students responded to the teacher. The students had one side of the class do nothing and be non-responsive. The other side nodded, smiled, and paid rapt attention. Soon enough, the students had the teacher sitting on a heater on their target side of the classroom.

When I talk about leading the conversation, I mean that you can do certain things to create rapport and connection.

When I say notice what's working, I'm talking about becoming a gentle detective. You learn to ask gentle questions and listen—and to detect people's personality style.

A powerful way to make a connection is to use insights related to Personality Styles. Authors Tony Alessandra, Michael O'Connor, Nicholas Boothman and Roger Dawson have discussed personality styles. In what follows, I put my own spin on the research.

In conveying this material over the years, I have found that using images related to animals makes these insights more memorable.

First, I'll give you a brief sketch of the **four Personality Styles.**

Lion: A hard-charging leader who may be considered abrupt or bossy.

Dog: A supporter who likes routine and cares about the feelings of others. This person may be slow to accept change.

Peacock: An extrovert who loves to stand out in a crowd and gain approval. This person may be ineffective when it comes to follow-up.

Beaver: An analytical person who likes tables, graphs and lots of details. This person wants to appear intelligent and slowly makes a decision (due to a great fear of making a mistake).

Now, I'll give you a preview of how the insights related

to Personality Styles can help you make a great first impression—which is a great connection.

The Lion (leader-type) fits well with the Dog (supporter-type). Susan knows that she has the supporter-style (or Dog personality style). She knows that she tends to be attracted to the Lion style. In fact, she has just started dating Mark, a man who is a classic hard-charging leader (Lion).

Susan also knows that Lion-style people subconsciously fear weakness and indecision in themselves. Also, Lion-style people become irritated when they encounter weakness, indecision or time-wasting in other people.

Here's how Susan shines with her knowledge of Personality Styles.

1) She does not hesitate when choosing what she wants from the dinner menu.

2) At other times, she offers supportive comments to Mark, such as: "That sounds like a good decision." "I appreciate how you pointed your team in an effective direction."

"Decision" and "effective" are important buzzwords for the Lion.

On the other hand, Susan's usual habit (with women-friends) is to hesitate and take some time when ordering from a dinner menu. This has become a running joke in the group of Susan's women-friends. But Susan wants to develop emotional connection with Mark before she unleashes her foibles.

An interviewer asked, "So people are attracted to those who have opposite personality styles?"

"Often, it is a matter of opposite temperaments attract," I replied. "But for long-term relationships, the couple needs to share similar values. Many of us have met happy couples in which one is the leader and the other is the supporter. Or one is neat and the other is messy. What counts is whether the two people share values like donating to charities or wanting two children."

The Lion and the Dog are a good combination. As author Nicolas Boothman notes they become a captain and willing crew. On a family vacation they will not be two captains knocking heads, disagreeing about every detail.

The fastest way I can convey the four styles—Lion, Dog, Beaver and Peacock—is by using the tables on the next few pages.

Please note this important point: we all have some of these traits. The secret is to let your compatible traits show when in the presence of the new person. This creates initial harmony and warmth.

The use of insights related to Personality Styles is part of a process called Impression Management. We can use Impression Management when we uncover the new person's personality style and put our best foot forward by demonstrating our similar traits.

An interviewer asked, "If you only show your similar traits, aren't you acting like a manipulator?"

"The most important detail is your intention," I replied. "It's reasonable to seek to make a good first impression when your goal is a new friendship. Later, after there is some initial harmony, you can express your True Self appropriately. In other words, we might all occasionally dribble food or something on our clothes, but no one would quibble with the idea of putting on a clean shirt before meeting someone or having a job interview."

The following paragraphs have ideas that focus on business interactions. I am including these ideas here to give you a quick overview of how personality styles interact.

In the following section:

Step 1: View details of each personality type
Step 2: Circle the behaviors you will use
(The following sections include some concepts noted by authors Tony Alessandra, Michael O'Connor, Nicholas Boothman and Roger Dawson.)

The Lion Personality Style

Characteristics: Fast-talker, finishes your sentences; talks primarily about results; hard-charging; blunt.

What excites them? Action.

Greatest Asset: Can out-accomplish anybody.

Greatest Failing: Can't stand weakness.

Greatest Fear: Being "Soft."

Unspoken expectations:

1) Wants you to interact with her in a quick, to-the-point way.

2) Wants to see results.

3) Would appreciate your having an agenda when you meet with her.

4) Would appreciate your coming up with three possible solutions and asking for her decision if you notice a problem.

5) Wants to see the bottom line.

What to Do to Make a Great First Impression (upon the Lion):

- Write notes and rehearse them before meeting.
- Interact in a quick, to-the-point way (with a written agenda).
- Show you are also strong; that is, you are unruffled by circumstances.
- Emphasize results and the bottom line.
- Come up with three possible solutions for a problem and ask for the person's decision.
- Demonstrate that you are one of the person's top producers.

When working with a Beaver (analyzer-type)...

The Beaver Personality Style

Characteristics: Massively detail conscious; wants to know the in-depth facts; often slow to make a decision.

What excites them? Reason.

Greatest Asset: High-quality work.

Greatest Failing: Too critical.

Greatest Fear: Appearing irrational.

Unspoken expectations:

1) Wants to see the in-depth facts.
2) Wants you to be thorough.
3) Would appreciate the graphs.

What to Do to Make a Great First Impression (upon the Beaver):

- Show that you're producing high-quality work.
- Show that you approach things rationally.
- Present in-depth facts and graphs.
- Appear to take your time in coming up with a decision.

When working with a Dog (supporter-type)...

The Dog Personality Style

Characteristics: People-oriented; considered friendly; a good team player; often slow to make a decision; hates pressure.

What excites them? Feelings generated by being around people who have similar interests.

Greatest Asset: Helpfulness.

Greatest Failing: Slow decision-maker; avoids pressure; unable to say no despite having too much work.

Greatest Fear: People being unhappy.

Unspoken expectations:

1) Would be interested in the people factor: how a proposal will be accepted by the team and how individuals

will be affected.

2) Wants you to be friendly, taking a few moments to chat person-to-person; has concerns about how you fit in with the other team members.

What to Do to Make a Great First Impression (upon the Dog):
- Show that you have similar interests.
- Demonstrate, via your words and actions, that you're not a source of pressure.
- Avoid pushing too much in striving for the answers you need.
- Show that you are happy as a team member.

When working with a Peacock (promoter-type)...

The Peacock Personality Style

Characteristics: Fast decision-maker; likes to be the center of attention; wants to feel good; doesn't like all the detail work; often has poor follow-up.

What excites them? Tossing around ideas.

Greatest Asset: Fun to be around.

Greatest Failing: Being erratic.

Greatest Fear: Not being liked.

Unspoken expectations:

1) May expect you to handle the details.

2) Would like to know that you like her (through small gestures).

3) Would expect you to listen to her if she's tossing around ideas.

4) Would like it if you helped with follow-up.

What to Do to Make a Great First Impression (upon the Peacock):
- Help with the details.
- Show (in little ways) that you like the person.
- Demonstrate that you're listening when the person is tossing around ideas.

- Help with follow-up tasks.

Now that you have had a chance to read an overview of the personality styles, I am going to talk about good combinations and subconscious attraction.

Subconscious Attraction

As I mentioned, the Lion and Dog tend to be a good combination. For example, some Lion individuals may feel a subconscious attraction to the Dog style because of his traits: "He's so calm. He's so alive. He lives in the moment." A Dog might be subconsciously attracted to the Lion: "She's so strong and confident."

Another good combination can be the Beaver and Dog. The Dog might say, "That's a good plan. I'm glad that you figured that out. You're so good at this." This is music to the Beaver's ears. The Beaver then feels something along these lines: "I feel better about me when I'm with you. You confirm that I'm intelligent and correct."

The Peacock and the Dog form a good combination. Some Peacocks are known for having poor follow-up. That's when having a partner who is a Dog helps. The Dog might say, "Oh, honey, you asked me to remind you to call Sara when we get home."

Staying Truthful

To make a great connection with a new person, you sincerely express appreciation for that person's positive natural tendencies. Earlier I mentioned the True Self, which is made of one's natural brilliance. Your True Self knows how to connect. What that means is that after you create initial harmony, you can express some heartfelt details in an appropriate way.

A number of spiritual paths hold that we are all connected to each other. It is only the Ego (or False Self), which keeps us distracted by fear, and self-preoccupation, which holds us back from paying attention and expressing supportive comments. The True Self wants to create harmony. In fact, the True Self may be the source of your desire to learn to be a better communicator.

As I mentioned earlier, our focus is on making a great connection (which facilitates a great first impression).

So demonstrate your appreciation. For example, in the honeymoon phase of courtship, we store good feelings in an emotional bank account. When an error occurs (like forgetting to call), there are extra funds in the emotional bank account for us to draw upon.

A Special Key: Identify your own personality style and avoid pitfalls.

When talking with a Lion, the Dog needs to avoid annoying traits like indecisiveness and weakness, which bother a Lion. We understand that the Lion dislikes weakness in herself or himself. That's partly why the Lion became a leader. Debbie Ford, author of *The Secret of the Shadow*, points out that we become something (a leader or follower) as a reaction. For example, Mark became a leader because he suffered abuse as a child. In order to prevent painful incidents from happening to him again, or from happening to others, Mark became a leader.

On the other hand, we need to realize that the Dog is strong in other ways. The Dog is firmly aware of the impact on people's feelings. The Lion can learn from the Dog how to have good relations with people.

Once there is some form of commitment in a relationship, partners start to appreciate the idea of different and not wrong. They start to appreciate how they are jigsaw puzzle pieces that fit together.

The Lion needs to walk carefully if he or she seeks to win the heart of a Dog-style person. The Lion does well to ask about the Dog's feelings first. Ask "How was your day?" before you pour out your ideas and travails of your own day. If a Lion fails to listen first, the Lion can be termed "self-absorbed," "a steamroller" or even "heartless."

Similarly, Daniel Goleman, author of *Social Intelligence: The New Science of Human Relationships,* writes about how we are designed for sociability and are constantly engaged in a neural ballet that connects us, brain to brain, with those around us. For example, in a speed-dating situation, it is better to ask gentle questions and listen rather than to attempt to impress the new person with your big accomplishments.

Lead the Conversation with Positive Questions.

As you ask questions and listen, you are like a gentle detective. You are discovering what personality style the person has, and you are discovering what is most important to him or her.

You can ask questions like:
- What's been going well for you?
- What are you looking forward to?
- What friendly comment has someone said to you?
- Tell me about something that went well and made you feel good ...

When the person responds, you get clues like:
- My project at work went well. The team really understood the critical point when they saw my graph. (This person is likely a Beaver—an analyzer.)
- I'm looking forward to our extended family gatherings. It's great fun to hear what people have been up to. (This is likely a Dog—a supporter.)
- My supervisor said that I found the key to impressing our new client. (This is likely a

Peacock—a promoter.)
- My team has been using the effective XYZ process. This has increased our bottom-line by ... (This is likely a Lion—a leader.)

Remember to express sincere appreciation for a new person's positive natural tendencies, which are visible as his or her personality style. This helps us make a great connection. Also, we learn to reduce the expression of our annoying habits (annoying to the new person's personality style). When we do this, we give the blossoming friendship a chance!

Principle:
Lead the conversation with positive questions.
Power Question:
What positive questions feel comfortable to you?

CHAPTER 18:
ENGAGE DEFINITE MOVES

5. Engage Definite Moves

Overcome Rapport-breaker #5: Avoid Hesitating (Coming Across as Not Confident and Not Having Anything Valuable to Offer)

Ever notice that confident people move in a confident manner? They make definite moves. They walk with good posture and ease. They move their hands and arms in ways that project competence.

In my workshops, I ask people to practice walking up to other attendees, who are portraying strangers gathered in conversation. I point to an invisible circle on the floor. This invisible circle is where everyone who is in the conversation group stands. Someone who stands tentatively and uncomfortably outside the invisible circle will look not confident and will appear to have nothing of value to offer.

That person will look like an outsider. It's better to walk like a confident person. Approach the group. Smile and stand in the invisible circle. Nod your head while listening to the person who is talking. Then ask him a gentle question. Some of my clients ask, "What if I'm too shy to ask a question?"

"This is where rehearsal comes in," I reply. I guide my clients to practice questions like:

- That sounds helpful. How did the idea come to you?
- That must have been frustrating. What happened next?
- That sounds like it worked well. Oh, I'm Tom, and you are ...?

Remember, a confident person would offer her name in a friendly, straightforward manner. Yes, it requires rehearsal. While driving to an event, you can rehearse by talking out loud in the car. Actually saying the words out loud is vital for you to develop confidence.

Recently, I received a phone call from a happy workshop participant. She said, "Tom, I applied the method I learned in your workshop. I acted as if I were a confident person at a social event at work. I started conversations. That was new for me."

Successful people learn to go ahead even when they feel like imposters, knowing that they will gain confidence and whatever else is required along the way. —Pamela Gilberd

Acting in the manner of a confident person may feel like being a fake at first. But the truth is that there is a part of you that is confident. We seek to honor that part of you—your True Self.

Action seems to follow feeling, but really, action and feeling go together; and by regulating the action, which is under the more direct control of the will, we can indirectly regulate the feeling, which is not. —William James

From William James's comment, we realize that our actions can help us to transform our experience—and ultimately how we feel about things.

Everybody should do at least two things each day that he hates to do just for practice. —William James

Practice! Eventually you will express yourself in ways that convey confidence. With enough practice, you start to express your True Self appropriately.

Earlier I mentioned the process of Impression Management. Impression Management is how we improve the first impressions we make by identifying a) our goal, b) the problem and c) the solution.

- Our goal is to help people see us as trustworthy, competent, caring and humble. (Authors Jo-Ellan Dimitrius and Mark Mazzarella have focused on these particular virtues.)
- Our problem is that we have a few natural tendencies that undermine the impression that we are trustworthy, competent, caring and humble. These unresourceful tendencies can be labeled toxic traits. Toxic traits lead to a bad first impression.
- However, our solution is to focus on the antidotes for the toxic traits.

To illustrate this process, our example is Stephen with his kind voice and gentle style of speaking. He is viewed as caring. His gentle manner and waffling style of speaking appear as a toxic trait. He comes across as too humble and as a weak leader. Also, because people sense that he is reluctant to push team members, they find him untrustworthy. Stephen's antidotes are to a) look people in the eye; b) talk directly (for example, "I need this work area cleared. Please pick up the stray materials and place them in the recycle bins. Thanks."); and c) lower the pitch of his voice.

Impression Management is a balancing act.

When teaching these skills at Stanford University, I emphasized that making a great first impression is also a balancing act. For example, when Susan is asked about a new employee, she responds, "Janet is sharp. And she seems to be a nice person." Clearly, Janet has conveyed her competence. And for good balance, she appears to be a nice person. If you ask someone what the traits of a nice person are, you'll hear, "courteous, respectful, friendly —and has a nice appearance."

Go-getters need to take special care not to be perceived as "good, but arrogant" or "bottom-line oriented, but doesn't seem to care about people."

When working with my clients, I help them discover their default-settings. Default-settings are like two-edged swords: they cut in good ways and in bad ways. The solution is to compensate for the undesirable perceptions that can result.

Know your tendencies and compensate for them.
— Tom Marcoux

Your Default-settings and Antidotes

We can use Impression Management when we uncover our natural tendencies, or Default-settings, that lead to toxic traits. Our solution is to focus on the antidotes for the toxic traits.

In the following paragraphs:

Step 1: Circle Your Default-setting

Step 2: Circle Antidotes You Will Use

(Some of the concepts in the next paragraphs have been noted by authors Jo-Ellan Dimitrius and Mark Mazzarella.)

Your goal is to be seen as having the following attributes.

Trustworthy

Default-Setting
(Toxic traits: Stop doing these actions):
- Shy.
- Avoid eye-contact.
- Soft-spoken.
- Speak too quickly.
- Move too quickly.
- Antidotes
- (Do these actions)
- Look at the bridge of the other person's nose.
- Speak louder.
- Practice with a friend, noting the speed of your movements.

Competent
Default-Setting
(Toxic traits: Stop doing these actions):
- Downplay your achievements.
- Give all the credit to others.
- Antidotes
- (Do these actions)
- 'Sprinkle' an occasional comment about something that worked for you.
- Talk about the team's accomplishments; give credit where it is due, and briefly mention your participation.

Caring
Default-Setting
(Toxic traits: Stop doing these actions):
- Speak about yourself too much.
- Antidotes
- (Do these actions)
- Ask gentle questions.
- Ask, "How can I be supportive of what you're

doing?"

Humble

Default-Setting

(*Toxic traits: Stop doing these actions*):
- Talk too loudly.
- Talk too quickly.
- Gestures are too emphatic.
- Appear overly enthusiastic (like a bulldozer).
- Antidotes
- (Do these actions)
- Mention a situation in which you learned something.
- Talk about what you are in the process of learning.

Special Note: If you appear too humble, you may be perceived as not being competent. Also, be careful about tooting your horn too loudly, because the appearance of arrogance will torpedo a great first impression.

Remember to act as if you are confident. Ask yourself, "What would a confident person do in this situation?" and "What would I do if I felt confident right now?"

Please see my book, *10 Seconds to Wealth*, for a discussion about real confidence. It will likely surprise you!

If you want a quality, act as if you already have it ... If you want a trait, act as if you already have the trait. —William James

Principle:

Act in the manner that a confident person would act.

Power Question:

What would a confident person do in the same situation?

CHAPTER 19:
CLOTHE YOURSELF AS A TRUSTED ADVISOR

6. Clothe Yourself as a Trusted Advisor

Overcome Rapport-Breaker #6: Avoid Dressing Inappropriately

In four seconds, how many judgments does a new person have about you? Fifteen.

When I give my presentation, "Now You See Me: Make a Great First Impression—Use Secrets of Power Networking," I discuss how a new person judges us based on our clothing. The person throws us into a category.

Categories include: professional, leader, artist, scattered-person, counter-culture person or some other category.

Roger Mellot, speaker and author of *Stress Management for Professionals,* mentioned how it is inappropriate to sell tractor equipment when wearing a tuxedo. The way to dress is in the form of a trusted advisor.

If you wish to network with affluent people, dress like the people they trust: successful business advisors and others.

If you want to attract someone in a high-income bracket, save your money for one or two terrific, expensive outfits.

Some people protest: "Can't I be myself?" Sure. Which part of yourself do you want to express? Your hung-over Saturday morning self? Or your job interview self? Or something in between?

Other people protest: "Clothe myself as a trusted advisor? I want a mate not a client!" Oh, really? Your potential mate wants to be able to trust you. You will be the person that your mate will depend on the most.

My point here is to take care with your clothing. For example, I have a friend who used to prefer to dress in jeans. Now she chooses very colorful dresses. These dresses convey an affinity for artistic pursuits. But she still looks "dressed up."

At the college where I teach, one woman, an instructor, was talking with another, saying, "I wore a suit yesterday, and everyone treated me better. I might wear a suit tomorrow!"

Earlier in my life, I wore a tie. My sweetheart teased me about it. When I wore that tie people treated me in respectful ways because of it. Also, I used my tie and dress shirt as a counterpoint to my speaking style which was comfortable and often casual. I came across as both professional and warm. (This is a detail my team members have observed on rating sheets of my speeches.)

Principle:
Dress like a trusted advisor.

Power Questions:
Which type of clothing do you feel helps other people consider you as trustworthy? Do you want to have a selection of different outfits for different situations?

CHAPTER 20:
TARGET LISTENING-MODE FIRST

7. Target Listening-Mode First

Overcome Rapport-breaker #7: Avoid Talking Too Much About Yourself

How can you inspire someone to enjoy talking with you? You ask a gentle question and start listening. People love to be heard. They are nearly dying of thirst—the thirst to be heard.

In my workshops, I lead participants to practice saying, "Hi! I'm [first name]. And you are …?" This process gets you into Listening-Mode quickly.

When you're listening, you're creating rapport.

Ask gentle questions to keep the rapport going.

Gentle Questions:

a. "Hi. I'm [first name]. And you are …?"
b. "Who is your ideal client?"
c. "What are you looking forward to?"
d. "How can I be supportive of what you're doing?"

Some of the questions above work best at networking events. Here are other questions:
a. How do you know our host Sam?
b. What is working for you at this conference?
c. Have you tried the chicken casserole?
d. So what brings you to this seminar?

Earlier, I mentioned the process, sprinkle a detail. It is true that it helps to mention a key, interesting detail about yourself in the conversation occasionally. But we want to ask another gentle question soon—to return the light of the conversation so it shines on the other person.

Patricia sprinkled a detail by saying, "I'm looking forward to seeing next month's issue of *XYZ magazine*. I just had an article published there. I'm really excited about it. So ... what are you looking forward to?"

We notice how she merely sprinkled the detail and avoided going into a monologue, expressing all her accomplishments.

It is helpful to look beyond one's accomplishments for one's identity. If you're not your accomplishments, what are you when you're meeting a potential mate?

You can be someone who truly provides value to a new person. How?

You can be:
- a warm person listening intently to what the person is saying
- a supportive person expressing appreciation and letting the person know she is important

Hold these ideas in your mind while meeting a new person.

Mary Kay Ash, founder of Mary Kay Cosmetics, the billion-dollar company, said, "When I meet someone, I imagine her wearing an invisible sign that says, 'Make me feel important!'"

To help convey your interest, lean forward a bit. This alerts your body to pay attention. In a previous chapter, we noted William James's words, "If you want a trait, act as if you already have the trait." To make a great first impression, ask in the manner of a good listener. Take a deep breath before you reply so that you can see if the person has indeed finished. Lean forward like a good listener. If the person says something and you have a reflex negative response, tell yourself, "I'm listening. I'm hearing the person out. This doesn't mean I'm agreeing. But I'm expressing compassion by listening."

Let's remember to ask questions and listen intently.

Principle:

Avoid talking too much about yourself. Ask questions and listen.

Power Question:

What questions will promote your comfort and the other person's comfort?

CONCLUSION OF PART 1 (BOOK III)

In Part I, we have learned to use the C.O.N.N.E.C.T. methods:

C — Come across with life
O — Open with a smile
N — Nurture positive stories
N — Notice what's working
E — Engage definite moves
C — Clothe yourself as a trusted advisor
T — Target listening-mode first

We have learned to honor each other's personality style and natural brilliance.

We have learned that a great first impression

is really a great connection.

In the next section, we go to the site of much seduction: the dating process. Turn the page and learn how to use the positive power of seduction.

BOOK III—PART II ... TURN SEDUCTION-POWER TO GOOD (USE EFFECTIVE DATING SKILLS)

Introduction

Have you ever said, "There must be an easier way"? The good news is that in Book III—Part I, we discussed how to make a great connection, which is an essential part of making a great first impression.

Now in Book III—Part II, we will explore the site of much seduction: the dating process. You will learn positive and effective dating skills. This relates to "turning the power to good" (the subtitle of this book). The skills in this section can help you eliminate wasted time and some heartache. In dating we want to lead with both our head and our heart.

One of my team members asked, "What about the readers who are married or in a long-term relationship?"

"We invite married people to continue courting and to brush up their dating skills to warm up their relationship with their spouse," I replied.

Let's return to the idea of being skillful with our head and heart. One of my clients had scheduled a get-together after work with someone he had just met. During the get-together, a problem emerged. She was talking about expensive cars; he wanted to talk about ideas and art. It became clear that they did not have a common ground. But stopping the interaction at that point would have been awkward. He felt that she wanted to continue the date through dinner, but he wanted to find the nearest exit.

Using effective dating skills often calls for scheduling a

first get-together for coffee at 1:30 p.m. on a Saturday afternoon. If the interaction does not go well, either person could gracefully end the meeting half an hour later.

A number of people report that getting stuck on a blind date can be excruciating. Using the dating method I just described, you can avoid such discomfort and loss of time.

To explore effective dating skills, we will use the D.A.T.E. process:

D — Devote
A — Ask
T — Target
E — Express

Let's continue ...

CHAPTER 21: DEVOTE

(The first method of D.A.T.E.)

Devote is a powerful idea. It has the air of love within it. It also contains the element of choice.

Roy O. Disney, brother of Walt Disney, said, "Decision making is easy if your values are clear."

In the introduction to this section, I mentioned that a first get-together for coffee at 1:30 p.m. on a Saturday afternoon may be best. If the interaction does not go well, either person could gracefully end the interaction at 2 p.m. The idea is to make the encounter pleasant and brief if there is no chemistry. In this way, you can make a friend or at least keep the interaction neutral. The more friends you have, the greater the number of possible referrals to people who may be a suitable partner. You get more choices.

My point is that we want to make good choices about how we devote our time, energy, and attention.

If you feel nervous before a date, devote some effort to rehearsing ahead of time. Call a friend and practice gentle questions with your responses. It helps. I know.

An interviewer asked me, "How can you discover if someone is interested in you before you ask for a date?" This points to the value of dating as a group. You can attend sit-down dinners and get to know various people in a group setting. Later, if you see that your interaction with one person is promising, you can say, "It's been really fun talking with you. Perhaps we could get together and have a cup of coffee sometime."

The Power of Attention

It is valuable to choose how you devote your attention. Here is a secret for men: Do what she does but with a delay factor. After a few dates, if a woman gives a man a backrub, she will likely be delighted if he does the same for her. I'll never forget the delighted expression on Michelle Pfeiffer's face in a scene from the movie *Up Close and Personal*. The camera pulls back to reveal that she is not in the throes of a passionate embrace—No! Robert Redford is massaging her feet!

Remember the delay factor. If a woman says (when you are a couple), "I love you," the truthful reply of "I love you, too" is required. But two hours later, if the man spontaneously says, "I love you," it means much more.

Paying attention is crucial. One speaker mentioned that how people interpret a loving action depends on personal history. One person may have equated chicken soup with loving care. You could give that person tomato soup eight times in one day—and that person still would not feel loved.

We need to devote our energy to what feels like love to our new friend. Ask this question when appropriate: "Tell me about a time you felt totally loved. What happened?"

Principle:

Dating goes more smoothly when you are clear in making

choices—that is, how you devote time, energy and attention.

Power Question:

How can you gently ask questions and learn what feels like love to the new person?

CHAPTER 22: ASK

(The second method of D.A.T.E.)

How do you know what is working with the person you are dating? You learn to ask specific, gentle questions. Then you'll know how to make dates go well.

It is true that part of the thrill of a new relationship is the suspense: Does he like me? Did she have a good time on our last date?

But you have a lot at stake here. Don't leave things to chance!

Ask effective, gentle questions like, "What's most important to you about _____?" This is a versatile question. It can take the form of:

- What's most important to you about a good meal?
- What's the best part of a dessert to you?
- What's the most important part of having a good birthday to you?

You'll notice that these are What-questions. The safer questions begin with how and what. Skip questions that begin with "why." The reason is that a "why" question puts many individuals on the defensive. Or the person jumps out of his or her feelings and into the head—to make up reasons that sound rational.

If you see the person hesitate or if you have a feeling that the person is just trying to toss out any answer, then you can supplement the question with a gentle, "I really want to know."

The next tip may be appropriate after a few dates. Jack

Canfield, author of *The Success Principles*, emphasizes certain questions, such as, "On a scale of 1–10, how would you rate how our get-togethers are going?" and "What would make our next get-together a 10?"

This relates to our principle for this section: "Ask, look, listen and flow with the silence."

Let's face it! Some people are just not that talkative. My sweetheart is often that way. And this helps us—because as a speaker and writer, I truly appreciate what a great listener she is.

Some individuals who talk less are people who feel "put on the spot" when someone asks them a question or series of questions. During one of my presentations, "10 Best Kept Secrets of Persuasion Masters," a man asked me, "What do you do if your boss is a clam? He doesn't answer questions."

"We all communicate. Watch his face. Look at what objects he keeps in his office," I replied.

John Gottman, author of *The Seven Principles for Making Marriage Work* and researcher at the University of Washington, conducted research that demonstrated that we can learn much more about what people think by:

a) observing body language

b) watching facial expressions

c) viewing their bookshelves and the pictures on their walls

John Gottman felt that these observations tell us more than asking the person directly does. Many people reply with something that they think sounds nice and appropriate, and which may be untrue.

I want to add a word about looking at someone's bookshelves. I conducted an informal survey. Whenever I saw *The Road Less Traveled* by M. Scott Peck on a person's bookshelf, I asked, "Did you get the chance to read this?"

And the majority of people I asked said that they had not read the book. What does this tell us? Not much. The person might be busy. The person might be overly optimistic about what she will find time to read. This is only one among many possible clues…

That's why I emphasize: Ask, look, listen and flow with the silence.

Flow with the Silence

Contrary to the habits of keeping an iPod, radio, or television on at all times, researchers show that human beings tend to need some silence.

We need time to think. If you ask a question, be patient while waiting for the person's reply. Sometimes a person will call you the next day and say something like, "I've been thinking about your question. What I realize now is …"

One sign that two people are becoming a couple is that they can have occasional comfortable silences. For example, some couples enjoy a comfortable companionship in the relaxation of sitting in bed, reading the Sunday newspaper. They're reading different sections, but they feel that they are together.

The ability to flow with the silence is especially helpful if the person you are attracted to seems to be a person of few words.

Some men say "I love you" through actions. They schedule an oil change, or they fix the screen on the backdoor. If you say, "Thank you. That means a lot to me," you might see your whole house get a makeover!

Principle:
Ask, look, listen and flow with the silence.

Power Questions:
What questions feel comfortable to you? Note any ways you would like to modify these questions:

- What's most important to you about _____?
- In order for you to know that I am really supporting you, what has to happen?
- What's most important for our get-togethers to be fun for you?

CHAPTER 23: TARGET

(The third method of D.A.T.E.)

What is the most skillful approach to dating and searching for a mate? Target what you want. Then think about where people like that go. What events or classes do they attend?

Also we need to target: What do you want to feel?

My clients have noted that they want to feel the following:
- affection
- supported
- valued
- cherished
- effective

The idea of feeling effective has two parts. The first part is when one feels appreciated by a romantic partner. The new friend says, "Oh, you're so good at that." That comment inspires enjoyable feelings.

The second part is when the person feels that the new friend could help him or her live well or be more effective. It could be a related feeling: "Hey, she's really insightful. Wow! We have chemistry, and she could be the one! I'd feel proud if she were with me."

It is important to have both romantic chemistry and a true friendship.

Clients have expressed feelings such as:
- My husband is my best friend.
- I can count on my wife to tell me the truth so I can

grow from the experience.

I mentioned that you need to target the suitable characteristics of a potential mate and to identify where that person might be. For example, one of the best relationships I have experienced (and we're still friends eleven years later) began when I met a woman at a spiritual center.

Here are questions about the suitability of a potential mate that you can answer in your journal.

- Is the person kind?
- Is the person respectful?
- Does the person keep commitments?
- Is the person flexible?
- Does the person flow with surprises that pop up in life?

A number of researchers have noted that people find kindness to be a key ingredient for a successful and happy long-term relationship.

Writing in your journal about your interactions with a new person can save you time and grief. When you write about the person's specific behavior, it sometimes becomes easier to see the writing on the wall. That is, you might realize that the person has demonstrated troublesome tendencies, such as failure to keep commitments or intolerance of little irritating things that arrive in life.

An old phrase goes, "If you don't know what you want, you won't get it."

Also remember, "Don't fall in love with someone's potential."

At the same time, we need to remember that each person is a package deal. The loving, kind husband may not be adventurous. In a marriage, a woman may need to do the research about a cruise or a Club Med program or a vacation in Hawaii. The loving, kind husband will probably go along with the plan, although he would not have the tendency to initiate such an activity.

In her book, *Why Talking Is Not Enough,* author Susan Page holds up a great model for a terrific marriage. She calls it a Spiritual Partnership. She writes, "Spiritual Partnership is a new model for couples, a different understanding of the purpose of loving relationships and how they work .... In Spiritual Partnership, you stop putting attention on your partner and start putting it on yourself. Your actions arise out of your own desire to become a more spiritually developed person."

The goal is to use powerful methods to bring a relationship to a higher, more loving level.

Attracting your ideal partner is helped if you nurture your own personal, spiritual growth. I invite you to seek my book *10 Seconds to Wealth: Master the Moment Using Your Divine Gifts.* The idea is that when you work on your own issues, you can attract more love and abundance into your life.

After you have been dating someone for a while, it is likely that you will notice annoying traits. Susan Page talks about the power with which one can "act as if." Susan mentions the example of a married couple: "When Becky started behaving as a loving wife and focusing on [her husband] John's strong points instead of his weak points, he was pleased and began to respond in kind. Becky also started to take better care of herself in the relationship and stopped depending on John for things he would never provide." The idea here is that Becky began to "act as if" she felt loving toward John.

At the beginning of a relationship, we may not feel much annoyance over our new friend's weak points. But we need to nurture ourselves continually. Then we can have reserves of patience for tough times.

Also, I have seen a number of couples in which one partner is "the neat one" and the other partner is "the messy one." Successful couples find a way to accommodate the quirks of both partners. The messy person gets his or her own study, and the neat partner is sure to keep the door to that room closed.

I invite you not to cross someone off the list because he or she demonstrates a trait that is merely annoying. However, any violence or verbal abuse is a primary red flag, and people are advised to get away from those who demonstrate these detrimental behaviors.

When you target what you want, being aware of your non-negotiables is valuable. These are details that you feel are deal breakers. For some people, a non-negotiable is illegal drug use.

Other people may focus on positive requirements. For example, the person must be respectful in talking, have a similar spiritual path or feel the same about having children.

In your personal journal, write your list. "My non-negotiables are ..."

Good relationships are often between partners who have opposite temperaments but the same values. For example, one person may be talkative and the other, quiet; both are loving parents.

Also, sometimes we are surprised. I know a couple in which the husband is conservative, and his wife has tattoos and a belly piercing. He had no idea that he would develop a lifetime love with someone who—on the surface—seemed so different. Once again, opposite temperaments but the same values.

Where to Find a Romantic Partner

A number of people I know made the decision that bars

are not suitable for locating their ideal partner. Here are other places that might be suitable:
- church
- workshops
- spiritual retreats
- college
- adult education programs
- the Internet (I know a couple that met in a chat room and subsequently got married.)

Similarly, for years I have mentioned this example: Where can an actor meet producers and directors? At workshops about funding and distribution!

The most important idea is to target what you want to feel in the relationship.

Principle:
Target what you want to feel in the relationship. This will guide you to locations where you may find a suitable romantic partner.

Power Question:
What do you want to feel? How do you know that the person is likely to continue to help you feel that way? Do you want to feel appreciated, cherished, admired or something else?

CHAPTER 24: EXPRESS

(The fourth method of D.A.T.E.)

What needs to be present for a good relationship? To give your new connection a chance, you need to express "the good news."

Remember that some of the intense joy at the beginning of a relationship is how the new person opens up a new world of "I like myself better when I am with you."

You can express the following Four Keys to a Better

Relationship:
- appreciation
- admiration
- acceptance
- compassion

Love does not consist in gazing at each other but in looking outward in the same direction. — Antoine de Saint-Exupery

De Saint-Exupery's idea is truly helpful, and it leads to a question: How do you know you're both looking in the same direction? One of you must be sure to express the *Four Keys to a Better Relationship*. Again, these keys are: appreciation, admiration, acceptance and compassion.

Express your appreciation. Women can help a male companion feel like a hero. A man can help a woman feel like a princess (cherished).

Express your delight in what the person did; in this way, help the other person "win." The idea of "win" can mean a lot to men subconsciously.

Learn to say thank you in effective ways. Leil Lowndes, author of *Talking the Winner's Way*, adds a phrase such as, "[Thank you.] Oh I'm so happy you told me. I just got [these shoes]."

Express admiration. Many men have noted that they were conditioned as a boy to think "winning is crucial." The woman who wants to encourage a relationship with a man will often find that it helps to make it a game that he can win.

For example, I once asked my sweetheart: "What makes you feel special on Valentine's Day?" She replied,
- flowers
- a balloon
- chocolate
- a card

- dinner

I know that when I provide these items I am doing well. I call them the Fabulous Five. Of course, I would do even better by providing something that is delightful and surprising.

Some people might ask, "Wait a minute. If you have to ask, isn't that not romantic?" Well, I tend to like "chick-flicks" better than my sweetheart does. So yes, I am a romantic, but I'm not a mind reader.

Earlier in this book, I mentioned that researchers have noted that many men would like to be a hero to their romantic partner. For example, my sweetheart gave me a photo of us together. She used Adobe Photoshop to place a thought-balloon above the image of her head. The thought read, "My hero!"

She said, "I thought you'd like that."

Yes, I do!

How does a man know that he's doing well? He needs the woman to let him know! She needs to express delight when he does something right—or even "near right."

When I was getting my degree in psychology, I learned about the experiment mentioned earlier in which a pigeon was conditioned to peck at a bar. At first, the experimenters rewarded the bird with a food pellet for being near the bar. (That's my comment about "near right.")

This led me to think, Men are like pigeons! Reward them with your sincere praise, admiration and appreciation for making an effort.

Express acceptance. In her book, *Why Talking is Not Enough*, Susan Page wrote, "Accepting something doesn't mean you have to like it; it means you stop fighting it... [One advantage when you accept your partner instead of trying to change him or her is] you will be focusing on your own spiritual growth, viewing the "problem" as an opportunity to develop your inner peace, your ability to love and tolerate."

What does this mean to us when we're starting to date someone? It means that we have our eyes open to the person's endearing traits ... and we flow with some of the annoying traits. For example, if your new friend has the habit of consistently being 15 minutes late, bring a book!

If you are under extreme deadlines, you can tell the person: "If I don't see you by 2:00 p.m. [a wait of 15 minutes beyond the usual 15 minutes], I'll have to get back to work. I won't be waiting." In this example, you're not berating the person, and you are protecting yourself from inappropriate consequences.

Some people just don't find being punctual to be part of their personal lifestyles. We can say, "Oh, that's Sam being Sam." If you're having a dinner party, and you want people to be at the table at 7:00 p.m., you can tell Sam that 6:30 is the target time.

A man is rich in proportion to the number of things he can afford to leave alone. — Henry David Thoreau

Over the years, my father has often become frantic while packing before a vacation. On a number of occasions, I have guarded my inner peace by meeting my parents on the morning of the trip—at the train station.

Express compassion. Just about any person I have met could use more compassion in his or her life. It is especially sweet to feel compassion from a romantic partner.

If you want other people to be happy, practice compassion. If you want to be happy, practice compassion. — The Dalai Lama

One fast way that your new friend can feel your compassion is by your saying something like:
- It sounds like that was frustrating.

- That's intense. How did you get through it?
- That sounds painful. Is there some way I can help?
- That sounds complicated. Would you like me to listen for a while? You might want to bounce some ideas off me.
- That sounds painful. Would you like my opinion or would you prefer that I just listen?

Many of us feel like we're dying of thirst—a thirst to be heard.

What an incredible gift it is to be heard.

Remember that people form a solid romantic relationship when they feel, "I like myself better when I am with you."

Also, when you express appreciation, admiration, acceptance and compassion, you are building a loving relationship. You are on your way (with the suitable partner) to Spiritual Partnership. This is a wonder to behold and worth every effort. This I know deep in my heart—and I wish this blessing for you.

Principle:

Express that the person is doing things right, and you will be building up the relationship.

Power Question:

How can you express what is working so that the person experiences, I feel better about myself when I am with you?

BOOK IV:
USE STRATEGIES TO MAKE YOURSELF STRONGER (YOUR DEFENSE AGAINST MANIPULATORS)

Earlier in this book I discussed how you can free yourself from a trance that makes you vulnerable to manipulation. Now, I'm going to share with you additional methods so you can make yourself stronger and more resistant to falling into such a trance. I first explored these topics on my blog at www.BeHeardandBeTrusted.com

The Topics:
1. How You Can Strengthen Yourself in the Face of Criticism
2. How You Can Get Strong and Stop Triggers from Running Your Life
3. How You Can Decide to Take Advice or Move Beyond It
4. How to Get the Approval You Really Want
5. How to Make a Courageous Decision to Free Yourself
6. How You Can Get the Support You Really Need!
7. How Money is Spiritual: Feel Better, Get More, Move Forward
8. How You Can Release the Brakes So You Really Succeed!
9. How You Can Light a Candle when Things Look Dark—and Renew Your Energy
10. How You Can Handle Tough Moments—and Protect Your Day

1. How You Can Strengthen Yourself in the Face of Criticism

"She just doesn't have a kind word for me. She just criticizes me," Laura said about her friend Mindy. Have you noticed a number of people who have the habit of criticizing nearly everything? Has a loved one's critical remarks got you down? Now, you can strengthen yourself. Let's use the W.E.L.L. process:

W – Wonder

E – Enter a neutral space

L – Let go

L – Leave them alone

1. Wonder

When you're faced with someone hitting you with criticism, consider:
- I wonder how I am doing. Am I strong enough to be patient or do I need to step away?
- I wonder what I can learn here.
- How can I take my ego out of this?

Some criticism (on the job) must be faced with the calm strategy.

Other situations may invite us to focus on being the stronger person and avoiding "engaging in mischief." If we respond to negativity with negativity, we compound the upset feelings.

The ego (that part of you that feels vulnerable) wants us to feel secure and to feel acknowledged for "being right."

Here's a big thing to wonder about: "How can things be okay even if this person holds to his/her own opinion and never acknowledges me as 'being right'?"

When we live an authentic life (true to our personal destiny), some people will never understand us. So we discover times when we need to just move forward. We may be hurting but we can be hopeful.

2. Enter a neutral space

Enter a neutral space. Let's face it: our ego is what gets us into trouble. It gets us thinking that someone disagreeing with us means that they have power over us. Or that we're vulnerable or even stupid.

The idea is to "go neutral"—that is, you quiet your feelings (and your face) by telling yourself neutral ideas like:
- We're just different.
- There is no match here.

The idea of "there is no match here" is about

acknowledging you do not share values or concerns with the criticizer. Often, upon reflection, we discover that we do not share the same values or life experiences with the criticizer. So getting that person to agree is probably impossible and also, actually, irrelevant.

When you "go neutral", you offer no resistance, thus reducing the amount of energy you're expending. And you can even reduce the possibility of escalating the conversation into a pointless argument. You might say to the criticizer, "Maybe so. I'll think about it."

3. Let go

One time, a member of my extended family said a mean, criticizing comment to me. In times past, such a "zinger" would hurt my feelings. But this particular time, I just laughed and said, "Well, thanks for that one." And I gently but swiftly ended the conversation.

This was a new response for me. It was a surprising demonstration that I truly had let go of my attempts to justify myself in the presence of that person. The truth is, that person will probably never "understand me." How could he? He has never been an entrepreneur; he has never risked thousands of dollars to try products in the marketplace. He has never led 136 people (cast and crew) to complete a feature film.

By his tone and his word choice, this criticizer demonstrated that he thought that he is better than I am. To avoid reacting, I could tell myself something a bit soothing, "I am different." How is this soothing? It is like an affirmation of my independence and personal identity. "I am different." Not better. Not worse. Just different.

To be able to let go, it takes nurturing yourself with appropriate sleep, recreation, time with someone who is kind to you . . . and more. Basically, you must be the expert on taking care of yourself so that your usual state of being is one of calm strength. This is not easy, and I find that it takes a constant devotion of focus and effort. It's worth it.

4. Leave them alone

Sometimes, a workable solution is to "leave someone alone." That is, take some time away from that person. One of my clients realized that her friend (since high school) had become a frenemy (meaning both a "friend" and an "enemy"). Now, when they talk, they just upset each other. So my client said, "I'll give you some space. I'll see how you're doing in June (two months later)." My client discovered that during the "radio silence" time, she suddenly had an abundance of energy because she had escaped her frenemy's energy-vampire clutches. An energy-vampire, like a mythic vampire of horror fiction, is someone who lives off others. Instead of draining blood, the energy-vampire drains your positive energy and good feelings. Be on the lookout for energy-vampires who are subtle. Notice how you feel after you have an encounter with various people in your life. Decrease your exposure time.

Sometimes, the only solution about criticism is to guard your personal energy and create time away from the criticizer.

You can do well, even if you're finding that some people merely lob criticism at you. Remember the W.E.L.L. process is:

W – Wonder
E – Enter a neutral space
L – Let go
L – Leave them alone

Every person who strives to live a life of success and fulfillment will be criticized.

If you try to "hide" and live in a "non-offensive, small

way," you get criticized anyway. Why? Because some people criticize as a habit or as misguided help or as sport.

At least, be sure to be your own person.

Some Thoughts about Criticism—and Persuasion and Seduction

First, let's realize that criticism drains our energy. Why? Because by its essence it is about "What you're doing is wrong. You are wrong."

On the other hand, I'm not talking about feedback. I organize my life to gain plenty of constructive feedback, which is vital for excellent performance. For example, I have two editors per book that I write. But criticism drains our energy.

Many of us, upon receiving destructive criticism, feel depleted of energy and even our self-esteem takes a hit. At such a moment, you may feel vulnerable and can be specifically vulnerable to inappropriate persuasion or seduction. If the only supportive words you hear on a particular day are from a salesperson ("You look good in this suit"), you might buy a whole matching wardrobe! Or if you don't feel appreciated by your romantic partner, you might be vulnerable to having your emotions swayed by hearing some compliments from someone attractive at the office.

The real solution to being vulnerable to inappropriate persuasion or seduction is to give yourself regular "nutrition"—that is, create relationships in which you give and receive love, appropriate approval and support. Only by devoting time and effort to building your relationships will you be sure to fulfill your relational needs. Then you will have a metaphorical shield against inappropriate persuasion or seduction.

Stay strong. It's crucial.

2. How You Can Get Strong and Stop Triggers from Running Your Life

"Why can't you just back me up on this?!" Jonathan yelled, and his girlfriend Nancy winced. He didn't know that hearing one detail (about Nancy's father) would trigger a big reaction in him. A visceral childhood memory arose for Jonathan, and suddenly cortisol dumped in his bloodstream and his heart raced. Now, he was in trouble. His tone was disturbing Nancy and they were on their way into a bad argument.

Jonathan, like many of us, is unaware of triggers that are imbedded in his psyche.

This example can alert us that hidden triggers can impede progress from therapy or reading self-help books. Sometimes, people complain: "Why is it taking so long for me to get better?"

The truth is, we need to deal with triggers that cause automatic and reflexive reactions. It's time to H.E.A.L.:

H – Hear the trigger
E – Enlighten
A – Act to replace
L – Leap back

1. Hear the trigger

You can't heal what you don't notice. Perhaps, you've heard of the phrase, "Hear him out." That's what you need to do with a trigger. Pause. Pay attention to how you're feeling. Observe your behavior. Notice if you're upset. Ask yourself:

- What's going on here?
- Am I upset for the reason I think—or is there something else going on?

- What could that be?
- Has something happened now that has stimulated my brain and body to react? Is the reaction really about something from my past?

Hear yourself—that is, notice your thoughts and reactions. Without awareness or reflection, you may find yourself living in a reactive way to patterns from your past. It is as if the trigger knocks you back in time to reactions from your younger/weaker self. Since this situation can be a subconscious reaction, you might benefit from talking through the situation with a counselor.

2. Enlighten

When you answer the above questions, you start to shine light on dark corners, and those corners lose their power. Insight alone is not enough. But we need to start with questions. Then, we find some answers and prepare for appropriate action.

3. Act to replace

When you know your trigger places you into a negative feeling, you have a choice. What choice? You can choose to install an Empowered Response—instead of falling back into a reaction.

We're talking about setting up a new pattern so that you can respond and not simple have a "knee-jerk reaction."

To set a new pattern, you will engage in a process of taking action to create an Empowering Trigger Sequence (ETS). What kind of sequence? It's a behavior sequence that functions like this:

- Something happens [the trigger].
- You notice how you feel.
- You put your reaction "on pause."
- You use a Pre-set Empowered Response.
- You feel better.

Let's see how this applies to Jonathan's situation. Nancy mentions something about her father, and out of the blue Jonathan feels upset. He notices that but he also has an urgent need to avoid starting an argument with Nancy. (What need? How about love and harmony in their relationship.) He takes in a deep breath, in essence putting his reaction on pause. Then he remembers his "Pre-set Empowered Response" to sit down.

Upon sitting down, his emotions settle down a bit. More deep breathing and he is feeling a bit better.

I have now given you an example of an Empowering Trigger Sequence.

Now, I share a lighter example. Several years ago, I would run with my father. After each run, we'd stop at a convenience store and get an ice cream cone. Whoa! Stop! That's not a good pattern for me. That's like calories out (run) and put them right back in (ice cream cone).

What would be an Empowered Response? Drink some water and have an orange.

You see, the water and orange replace the ice cream cone.

If you take out a bad habit, you have a hole in your behaviors. Instead, set up an Empowered Response. In this way, you "act to replace" a reaction with an Empowered Response.

One of my editors of this book said, "You gave yourself an ice cream cone as a reward." I replied, "Good point. I decided to go deeper and find a reward that does not involve calories! One thing I like to do is soak in a hot bath and read an empowering book." Again, this process is about choosing an Empowered Response.

4. Leap back

Dealing with our personal triggers takes both time and perspective. We must leap back and away from our distractions and busyness.

Many of us are caught up in "being busy." Don't mistake activity for making progress. As I shared recently with my graduate students: learn to notice the difference between the urgent and the important. For example, a ringing phone is urgent. However, my keeping an appointment with myself to complete writing a graphic novel is important. Why? Because it is my goal to have a trilogy of graphic novels titled *Jack AngelSword*. This trilogy is important to me.

[If you're interested, you can visit "JackAngelSword" at Facebook.com.]

So now, I'm inviting you to focus on the important. Do you want to remain a "triggered person"? Or do you want to be strong and proactive? Learn to instill your own Empowering Trigger Sequence. Observing your patterns and developing positive responses are truly important to your quality of life.

To do this, you'll need to "leap back" — that is, you need to step back and observe your behavior. Does a particular behavior help you live well: healthy, whole, and enjoying abundance? If not, get to work and install an Empowering Trigger Sequence [You might need assistance from a counselor].

Part of "leap back" may be to install a Pattern-Interrupt. For example, one of my clients sits on the floor during a heated argument with a loved one. Sitting down helps my client to calm down. [As a side note: avoid saying "Calm down" when someone is upset. Has anyone calmed down when told to "calm down"? Unlikely. Some people "get triggered" by hearing "calm down" — they feel as if someone is trying to control them.]

Earlier, I mentioned how some people find the mere reading of a self-help book to be inadequate for real progress. Instead, be sure to do the exercises in the book, and consider getting training. [For example, I offer Home Study Courses. Many clients and graduate students enjoy my coaching them in effective speaking methods. They actually practice helpful methods.]

Your real power is in the choices you make of your own programming.

You'll be glad you took action to work on your triggers and behavior sequences.

And I'm cheering for you.

Some Thoughts about Triggers—and Persuasion and Seduction

Let's face it: Persuaders and Seducers love to press our triggers. What triggers? They can include words, gestures or phrases that get us reliving some past pain. For example, a seducer can place her hand on her target's face in just a certain way to trigger some old feelings. Maybe the way a past lover caressed him.

Why do Persuaders and Seducers seek to press our triggers? It gives them power and makes us vulnerable in the moment. We fall back (often) into some past pain that makes us pliable, distracted, and receptive to their influence. Protect yourself. How? Find out about your triggers. Make sure to set up an Empowering Trigger Sequence. Take action so that you program yourself to be strong (this whole book teaches you methods that empower you). Don't leave yourself open to the programming of some malevolent Persuader or Seducer. A number of people find therapy or counseling to be helpful so that they become aware of their trigger-points and how they can proactively deal with them. Sometimes therapy can be for a short duration or a longer one. Take actions to strengthen yourself.

3. How You Can Decide to Take Advice or Move Beyond It

When I heard my friend's delighted laughter, I replied and said for the first time: "Yes, I'm an Epiphany Coach. I help people get where they need to go by what's inside their heart."

Now, I have a question for you: When's it a good time to take advice? And when is it best to move beyond such advice? The label "Epiphany Coach" arose in my thoughts because I just helped a friend shape her speech and she experienced the joy of self-discovery. This was the source of her laughter. I asked certain questions and she found answers hidden inside her heart.

I'm telling you this story because I next sought advice and I needed to be careful about choosing whether to accept such advice or move beyond it. You'll also face dilemmas in which you can either greatly improve your life or stifle your growth by how you respond to advice.

When I said, "Epiphany Coach" the first time, I felt energized and on purpose. I went to my inner circle of advisors to hear advice about using that label (I'll tell you the result a few paragraphs below). To find your answer as to whether to take someone's advice, you need to H.E.A.R. yourself:

H – Honor yourself
E – Enter your inner world
A – Arrange to hear yourself
R – Realize

1. Honor yourself

It's your life. No matter what a friend, family member or even an expert tells you—no one can see your personal path. You must honor yourself and your own personal vision. What does it mean to honor yourself? It means, you need to celebrate that you are different from other people. You have different things that excite you, scare you, and even dare you. What amazing things await you, if you only dare step outside your comfort zone?

Much of the advice we hear tends to reinforce staying in comfort zones. For example, my father's advice usually revolves around "be careful," "don't upset people," and "don't get hurt." He retired from being a mail carrier for thirty years. He would agree that he has not one entrepreneurial bone in his body.

If I had followed my father's advice, I would not have attended the college I attended, directed the feature films I've directed, given the speeches across the United States that I gave and more. I won't talk about the band I was the lead singer for . . .

I'm so glad that I stepped out of my comfort zone and have enjoyed the adventures of my life. The adventures blossomed from my honoring my own personal vision.

2. Enter your inner world

Walt Disney's wife, brother (and partner) and the board of directors were all against creating Disneyland. Why? It was new. No one had seen a clean, wholesome theme park before. Walt's detractors could not enter the world of Walt's personal vision.

For many of us, we need to enter into a "new world" — the one of our own personal vision. How? Start with these questions:
- Where is the magic in what you do?
- Does this advice help you express your true and inner world?

To know the answers to the above questions, you must be aware and connected with your inner world. My clients find that writing in a journal is a valuable way to enter into their true and inner world.

3. Arrange to hear yourself

I talked with people in my inner circle about the label "Epiphany Coach." I did not just notice what they said—I noticed how I felt. The point is that you do not need to follow someone's advice. Instead, you need to notice how you feel as you hear yourself talk about a new idea. So why consult with my inner circle? Because it is a safe place for me to explore my thoughts and first impressions.

4. Realize

Realize that often you've got to be bold! The top successful people I have talked with have often said that they needed to take bold action on an idea arising from their intuition. They needed to move forward with their business endeavors—even when others did not agree with their ideas.

So when do we take someone's advice? Answer these questions for yourself:

- Am I honoring my own personal vision? Will this advice honor my vision?
- Do I know what my heart wants? Does this advice apply to that?
- Have I arranged to talk with people whom I trust and feel that I can speak my mind (and heart)? Do I listen to what I say and notice how I feel?
- Is this the time for bold action? Can this advice help me move forward?

So when I went to my inner circle and mentioned my thoughts about calling myself an "Epiphany Coach," a number of close friends did not like the phrase (for their personal reasons).

I reflected more on that title. Then I moved beyond that title to what really works for me: *Executive Coach and the Spoken Word Strategist.*

So what is the essence of making choices about how you handle advice? Remember to honor what is in your heart.

Let's face it. We're here to express the good and hopeful in our heart.

Express and share.

Some Thoughts about Being Careful about Advice—and Persuasion and Seduction

Persuaders and Seducers have advice for us, but they are clever in how they present it. Why? Because they know that advice can generally invite resistance. So how do Persuaders and Seducers present advice?—in the form of a story. The story can be a cautionary tale. A story gets beneath our defenses. We've been conditioned to enjoy and pay attention to stories since our childhood. While you're listening to a story, ask yourself, "Why is this person telling me this story? Are they really trying to help me—or are they trying to get something done for themselves?"

One of the toughest situations of dealing with advice occurs when your family member tries to persuade you to do something the adviser feels you should do. A loved one may try to dissuade you from a path that is truly your destiny. Why dissuade you? The person wants to stop you from making a mistake and getting hurt. The truth is that living authentically does involve appropriate risks at times [for more information about how to take appropriate risks, please see my book, *Connect*]. No one can know another person's true path. Only your heart has the true compass for your next step. We need to listen to our own hearts—regardless of a loved one's good intentions.

The important thing is to make time and space for you to calm down and think through a course of action—something I call thinkspace. This is always useful when dealing with a

Persuader or Seducer. You can say something to a Persuader like: "Oh, something has come up over here. I'll need to call you back."

What's going on here? You are giving yourself thinkspace to ask yourself the hard questions like:
- Is this person really on my side?
- What outcome is this person aiming for and what benefit does he/she want?
- Do I need to go to someone else—who is truly trustworthy—and talk through my thoughts and feelings about this?

Watch out to make sure that you're not particularly vulnerable to people who give you advice. And, remember that Persuaders and Seducers often use a story to avoid inciting resistance in you. Be sure to check with your own intuition first.

4. How to Get the Approval You Really Want

"Why can't she just let me be me?" Margie said to her friend Sarah. Margie's hopes kept being dashed each time she mentioned one of her new accomplishments to her mother. It just seemed that Margie's mother never had a kind word for her. Is there someone in your life from whom you'd like to receive some approval? Are you getting that approval?

Here are three valuable elements of a healthy approach to approval. We'll use the W.I.N. process:

W – Wonder
I – Invest in positive relationships
N – Nurture

1. Wonder

When you try to gain someone's approval and you don't get it, it can be a good time to wonder about what you're really aiming for. In talking with clients, I often hear that someone is looking for some type of safety. For example, if you seek the approval of your supervisor at work, you may be looking for some form of job security. And that can be a good thing. Early in my work life, I discovered that doing a good job did not guarantee keeping a job—particularly when 29 people and I were laid off after we helped a bank attain the status of becoming the first bank with online banking. "Thank you. Good job. Goodbye," said that bank's management. What does this mean? It means that the vice president's approval and statement of "Good job" ultimately did not mean job security.

So let's look at your journey about getting approval at work as strengthening your position. When you strengthen your position, you make sure that you have a strong personal brand and that management sees you as a vital asset to the company. But we cannot guarantee that we're "safe at that job."

One powerful idea I've heard is: "Job security is when you keep up your skills and your ability to get another job."

So yes . . . do praiseworthy work. Strengthen your position. Make sure that you carefully let management know that you're doing a good job. And realize that approval does not equal safety. It is something else. The truth is: you'll need to give yourself approval—that is, you need to know, in your heart, that you're doing a good job.

2. Invest in positive relationships

A good plan is to invest in friendships and relationships in which people "build you up." Some people (perhaps, because of their own personal life-difficulties) cannot cherish and support you in a kind way. Many of us try again and again to get a family member to give us approval. For example, a woman "Sarah" sought therapy from a counselor

I know. Again and again, Sarah tried to get support from her mother. Finally, the counselor said, "What? Did anything change? Doesn't your mother tend to say the exact thing to take the wind out of your sails?"

If you're faced with a similar situation, stop going to the wrong people for support and approval. Often the wrong people are referred to as "energy vampires." Make sure to limit your exposure to these drainers.

Instead, focus on devoting time and energy to those relationships that strengthen you.

3. Nurture

The simple truth (not an easy truth) is that we must nurture ourselves. Treat yourself in the way you would care for a close friend. How? You'd provide a good sleeping area for adequate rest, nutritious food and, probably, some recreation. When you take care of yourself (exercise, eat well, sleep, enjoy quiet time and a hobby), you will develop a reserve of energy. And—this is important—you'll probably stop radiating neediness. Sometimes, in friendships or in business relationships, people feel uncomfortable when they sense our neediness or desire for approval. Often neediness attracts subconscious resistance from other people.

On the other hand, nurture yourself and then people will feel good in your presence. Approval, like happiness, appears as a by product of living in a healthy way. We get ourselves tangled up when we make approval a goal. Live your life expressing your "aliveness" and creativity. When approval happens to arrive, enjoy it. We can make approval into something that we prefer instead of something that we try to "demand" from life. Approval from others really is like an occasional dessert.

So let's make life about giving and enjoying the moment. Let's face it. We subconsciously hope that approval will somehow make us feel better. We imagine that approval will be something to give us a bit of peace. Often, the approval that we seek won't give us inner peace. Ask any celebrity with a lot of fans: "Now, do you feel better and relaxed?" A number of celebrities have said that being famous has not given them what they were seeking.

What approval will give you that good feeling inside? Your own healthy approval. An old phrase is: "Happiness is something to do, someone to love and something to hope for." Make your life about expressing your authentic self and making a contribution to others—and healthy inner approval will blossom. That's when joy and fulfillment become part of your daily life.

Some Thoughts about Approval—and Persuasion and Seduction

Let's realize that many of us have been conditioned since birth to crave approval. Why? Receiving someone's approval feels good. There's an old phrase: "If Momma is happy, everybody is happy. If Momma is not happy, nobody is happy."

Whose approval do you need? The truth is: You need your own approval. I remember this quote:

When I do good, I feel good; when I do bad, I feel bad, and that is my religion. — Abraham Lincoln

Persuaders and Seducers use their approval of you as a way to manipulate you and get their way. The solution is to keep yourself strong. Do things, on your own, that strengthen you.

For example, I do work for various audiences. I write books, make feature films, write fiction, and give speeches. Because I work with a number of art forms, I feel a bit less pressure when some readers may not find a connection with my writing. I realize the truth that no performer can please everyone in the audience. I have a phrase: "I do it because I do it." What I mean is that I do my various forms of artwork because I get intrinsic joy in the process of being creative. For example, I'm enjoying the writing of this sentence on my birthday.

Be sure to enjoy your life so much that you don't let the pale thing of someone else's approval push you around. The more time you spend in misery, the more vulnerable you are to a Persuader's or Seducer's approval.

It's important that you feel good about your own actions. Experience your own approval.

5. How to Make a Courageous Decision to Free Yourself

"Your thinking is not right," Laura's mother said. Laura felt her throat tighten as if her mother's ever-present criticism was literally strangling her. Then Laura remembered my suggestion: "Get around people who encourage you, who build you up. Decrease your exposure to people trying to tear you down."

Laura said, "Something's come up here. I got to go—"

"What?! What could be more important than—?!" Her mother screeched.

Laura hung up the phone.

Now, I invite you to make the courageous decision: Decide to do what's necessary to strengthen yourself and to find a positive direction that is beyond your own ego's focus point. This process is about freeing yourself.

Each person feels down or lost on occasion. Here's an answer: turn your attention to living with integrity. According to the *Merriam-Webster Dictionary*, integrity means: "firm adherence to a code of especially moral or artistic values; incorruptibility; an unimpaired condition;

and the quality or state of being complete or undivided."

So the courageous decision is to walk your own path and experience the state of being complete and undivided. And allow others to walk their own path, too. Why? The simple truth is that people often don't want input from you or me. One way to help yourself feel okay about letting go is to focus on this phrase by author James Baraz: "I honor your life's journey."

And when some people habitually and consistently criticize you, make sure that you reduce your exposure to them.

Take care of yourself. Guard your own flame of life. Ask yourself these questions:
- Does this build me up?
- Is this tearing me down?
- Does this help me do something positive (with integrity) with my life?
- Does this give me strength?
- Does this drain my energy?

Then get away from energy-drainers. A draining influence could be a person, an upsetting news story, a draining movie or even a personal habit. Be sure to free yourself from such influences. Make a choice and take action: change the channel, take a walk, or enjoy quiet time.

We need people fully alive. Thanks for taking care of you and bringing more light and joy for all of us.

Some Thoughts about Courage to Walk Your Own Path—and Persuasion and Seduction

Our best defense against inappropriate persuasion or seduction is to have a fulfilling life. It takes courage to walk your own path because a lot of people merely conform to the latest trends of thoughts and interests. You need to be your own person. And that is an empowered stance to take in life. As you walk your own path, you'll probably discover that some people try to hold you down or push you around. Don't let them! Step away from them as much as possible.

You need to be sure to have many nurturing elements in your life. Why? If you're starving for support, you might reach out to a Manipulator, who appears to be a supporter. The Manipulators will take advantage of that. So be sure to have multiple supports in your life. Recently, I gave a speech in a large room and I noticed a number of pillars holding up the ceiling. Those pillars were necessary. Make sure that you devote time and effort to nurturing the "pillars" in your life: your friendships and taking care of your health. Stay strong.

6. How You Can Get the Support You Really Need!

"Why don't I get any help at home unless I get mad and yell?" Judy asked her friend Kira. Do you find yourself thinking something similar? Are there times when you feel that your loved one is failing to be kind and supportive of you? First, you need to nurture your own energy and avoid asking for help when you're already upset and overwhelmed. (I know, it can be tough. Life does move really fast — and we're all so busy.)

To be effective at asking for support, you need to be good at two things:

1. Emphasize Reciprocity
2. Express the Pure Intention First

1. Emphasize Reciprocity

How can you help your partner feel inclined to help you? It comes down to two words: give first.

People tend to be receptive after they have first received something positive. So the process of gaining support is really about a week-to-week lifestyle of mutual support.

How do you know what your partner would appreciate? Ask a gentle question: "In order for you to feel supported by me, what has to happen?" You can offer a possibility like: "Joe, how about I take the kids on Thursday night and you can see a movie with your friends, and how about you take the kids Saturday morning, and I'll attend an aerobics class?"

You'll feel supported when your partner does something in return. The truth is, people are so often distracted by their own problems that they fail to see what their partner needs or desires. Help your partner support you. Provide the ideas about options, then you'll find that you'll probably get the support you really want.

2. Express the Pure Intention First

One night, I was working away while my sweetheart was relaxing and watching TV in the next room. I was feeling overwhelmed and when she walked into the room, I felt like saying: "Where were you?"

Instead I said, "I missed you." That was expressing the pure intention first. When I say Pure Intention, I mean the kind and loving thought that creates connection between romantic partners.

On the other hand, saying "Where were you?" with an intense tone is a springboard to an argument.

I asked her how she felt about my saying, "I missed you." She replied, "Tom, I think you did a good job. It made me feel like I need to spend more time with you."

To express your Pure Intention, you need to first discover it yourself. My clients find writing in a journal helps. Again, your Pure Intention is the loving essence that you feel in a situation.

Above, I said that I felt like saying "Where were you?" This comment was something I call my first reflexive comment. Let me illustrate this for you. Have you ever seen two kids when one hits another on the shoulder? Like a reflexive reaction, the other kid automatically hits back.

When you want more support in your life, you don't let your reactions run your life. Instead, you become proactive. How? You learn to do something I call a Turnaround. You take your first reflexive comment and transform it, that is, you turn it around. Here's an example:

First Reflexive Comment: "Nobody helps me around here until I yell."

Turn it around. Revised Version: "I'd really appreciate some help. Would you rather take out the garbage or put some oil on the squeaky hinge on the backdoor?"

Why does this Turnaround process work? You do not attack. You gently offer two options and your partner chooses (ideally) one of them. Your partner is more likely to be agreeable if he or she feels in control. In this manner, you avoid activating any resistance in your partner.

Let's go through another example:

First Reflexive Comment: "You're not spending enough time with the kids."

Turn it around. Revised Version: "I feel Joey would like to play catch with you. How about I get take-out food while you take Joey to the park on Thursday or Friday evening?"

Some readers might say, "Yeah, that sounds good. But it seems complicated." or "How am I going to think of this in the moment?"

Good question. It takes preparation before you ask for support. The truth is: when you really want support, you need to be strategic in your methods of asking. (I provide more methods for getting support and for bringing financial abundance into your romantic relationship with my book, *10 Seconds to Wealth: Master the Moment Using Your Divine Gifts.*)

The science that underlies the process of a Turnaround is related to how we have mirror neurons in our brains. Mirror neurons are brain cells that are stimulated and that match the feelings of the person talking to us. This is the reason that you need to get into a positive state of mind before you ask for support. Then, your partner's mirror neurons will be stimulated in a positive way.

This means that you need to prepare before you ask for support. Revise your "first reflexive comment," rehearse saying the positive version, and then gently ask for the support you need.

Some Thoughts about Support—and Persuasion and Seduction

The Manipulator preys on people who do not have regular and consistent support in their lives. Why? Because the Manipulator likes to get what he or she wants in an easy way. You can see a person without support as a drowning person reaching out for a life preserver. The Manipulator jumps in and provides what looks like a life preserver—perhaps some approval, a compliment, or a favor. The Manipulator's effort is not genuine; it is merely a ploy so that the Manipulator ultimately gets a personal benefit.

The real defense is to devote time and effort to your primary relationships so that you keep them, like a car, well tuned. Many of us take great care of our cars. We note regular maintenance duties in our day planner or PDA. And we take action to keep our cars well tuned. To nurture your relationships, it also helps to use your day planner or calendar—and to take appropriate action, including listening, talking, quality time, fun activities and more. Then you won't be a drowning person (deprived of support). Then the Manipulator will not have an easy handle on you.

You will be stronger.

7. How Money is Spiritual: Feel Better, Get More, Move Forward

"He's a really nice guy, but he just can't seem to save any money," Nancy said describing her boyfriend Stephen. Later, she broke up with him and explained the situation as "I wanted a life partner, not another kid." Money is related to feelings of abundance, lack and fear (spiritual topics). As an instructor of college level Comparative Religion, I have discussed various topics that a number of spiritual paths address. When a person considers life as being full of possibility, she can see abundance as a possibility for her. This reminds me that Albert Einstein said, "The important question is: Is this a friendly universe?" Do you feel that the universe is friendly—that you have opportunities for good things in life? Are you grateful for what you already have? My personal affirmation is: "Money is a tool I use well for the benefit of all." And that's how my year goes. I hire a number of people to do various tasks, and we all benefit.

Do you feel somehow empty and you try to fill the void with stuff? This question brings us back to the two spiritual topics of lack and fear. People fear lack—lack of money, time, robust health or loving relationships. If we consider the universe a friendly place, we are likely to move forward and develop positive relationships with others—and even with ourselves.

Now, imagine that you have a metaphorical relationship with money. Let's take it a step further: imagine that money is just a symbol of the energy we exchange with other people. Now is the time for you to develop money skills and ease some pressure you experience around money. Let's start your journey to ease some money pressures by using

the N.O.W. process:
- N – Nurture your money skills
- O – Open your eyes
- W – Wonder about possibilities

1. Nurture your money skills

Many years ago, my father gained money in a settlement after a beverage truck had smashed his parked car. My father wanted to go on a family vacation. At the time, my schedule was full and I was heavily invested in my company's entrepreneurial projects so I suggested: "Dad, put the money in a CD and then we'll go in a month or two." My father didn't put the money aside. In fact, he spent it all on "stuff." We never went on that vacation.

My father never developed the skills of saving and using budgets. But this is *not* for you.

I made sure to take an opposite path from my father. I read a number of books about money skills. I learned about CDs, Roth IRAs, developing budgets, saving and more.

I invite you to experience something positive. If you will invest some time daily (even just 9 minutes) to learn about money skills, you will develop empowering feelings. When I discuss money skills, I'm talking about both pragmatic skills and whole person skills. Pragmatic skills include balancing a checkbook, composing budgets and sticking with those budgets. Whole person skills include approaching life with gratitude, shifting away from low moods, and developing interpersonal skills for better business relationships.

2. Open your eyes

Many of us get stuck in some disempowering money habits, but we don't pause and truly look at the situation. It's like dating the same type of person over the years. [In fact, I had to break myself away from that kind of pattern early in my dating years.]

Open your eyes and view your patterns about earning money and making purchases. For example, before I make a significant purchase, I talk the situation through with my sweetheart. She is insightful. This is part of my careful approach to expenditures.

Here is the secret: when you pay attention to your money details, you drop some free-floating anxiety, which is feeling uneasy but you don't have a concrete reason. Instead, when you pay attention, you know where you stand. You develop a step-by-step process of getting out of debt (if necessary). Open your eyes, make a plan, and take a step forward daily. You'll feel better.

Here's another thing to open our eyes about: to have an opportunity to earn more money, we probably need to press through fear. One of my clients was just offered an opportunity to do a new type of project. She has the skills, but she's afraid of the contract negotiation process. But she does have an edge: she gets coaching on how to talk about the contract and she rehearses. This process quiets down a good portion of her fear. Still, she has to press through fear to get the work and succeed in bringing more money into her life.

Needing to press through fear is not a failing. It's a fact of life. A number of authors have noted courage is feeling the fear and doing the work anyway.

So I invite you to keep your eyes open about where you need coaching and what you have fears about. Get the necessary coaching, rehearse, and move forward. It's worth it. And it will increase your net worth.

3. Wonder about possibilities

If you get stuck in thinking that your life will just be more of the same, you'll miss the opportunities for new financial abundance. Why? Because making more money calls for you to grow and try new activities. You need to make space for: "I wonder about . . . "

For example, you could supplement your income by turning a hobby into a source of income. Tina, who enjoys writing, might say, "I wonder if I wrote a novel whether some additional funds might come in." She'll never know until she takes action.

Steven, who builds websites as part of his job at a corporation, might say, "I wonder if I could start a side business and perhaps, get a couple of freelancers to help me offer website building services."

When we wonder about possibilities, new experiences can happen. It's true that we'll need to initiate the process by taking new action. But it's important to notice that action comes at the end of a 3-step sequence: thoughts lead to feelings which lead to action. It begins with the thought: "I wonder . . ."

Let me show a bit more about how we interact with money as a spiritual path.

My father has a favorite phrase: "It's hard to make money." That's like saying that one must struggle.

I do not agree with him. Effort is not the same as struggle.

I have chosen different beliefs that include:
- Money is a tool I use well for the benefit of all.
- I'm good at leading a team, together we create many wholesome benefits, and that process brings money flowing in.
- Serving people and receiving gratitude and energy (money) in return is good, healthy and spiritual.
- Higher Power guides me through my intuition in how to serve many people and this brings money flowing into my life and the life of my family.
- I'm a good leader, able to hire many people and

improve their lives and the lives of our customers.
- I release struggle. I put in intelligent effort and I gather effective people who devote intelligent effort, too.

I'll take this another step. The way I make money through my company begins with a vision:

We create encouraging, energizing edutainment for our good and humankind's rise.

– Tom Marcoux Media, LLC Mission Statement

So my spiritual view of making money is not that it is "hard" to make money. Instead, my view is making money takes thought, effort, humility to learn every day, courage, dedication to service, discipline to make a profit, and personal strength. It requires of me the discipline to be a good leader of myself and my team members. It is part of my spiritual journey.

Making money does not need to be "hard." For example, every month I make money with my books purchased on Amazon.com. I do not print the books and I do not ship them. The funds are automatically deposited in my company's bank account. It took my effort to write the books, plus the efforts of editors and book design team members. That was not "hard." It called for effort and persistence.

Money appears to be the source of a lot of distress in this world. But money is only a symbol of energy. What causes true distress? Greed and hunger for power with no self-restraint of compassion. And it is our personal thoughts and patterns that give money the power or pull it may have in our lives. Remember my affirmation: Money is a tool I use well for the benefit of all.

Some Thoughts about Money—and Persuasion and Seduction

Imagine that someone starts spending significant money on you . . . and that you grew up with not much cash. Many years ago, I went through that type of situation. I discovered that at first, it feels like much needed rain pouring on the parched desert. But soon, the person low on cash can start to become "too agreeable"—that is, he or she agrees to anything that the bill payer prefers. Which restaurant? The one that the bill payer likes.

Similarly, I remember a friend who lived with her doctor boyfriend. He paid the bills. Sure, she was attending college, but things were getting upside down. Things got better when she started working part time. She had her own money and she was contributing to the household bills. This helped her raise her own self-esteem.

Many people ignore their issues around money. To do so makes them vulnerable to being manipulated. Bestselling author Geneen Roth described how she suppressed her feelings about money, which led to her losing 30 years of life savings to the Bernie Madoff investment scheme. Geneen reports that if she had paid attention, she would have diversified her financial affairs or, perhaps, avoided the Bernie Madoff situation altogether.

I invite you to study how to be effective with earning and saving money. Money brings up life issues around abundance, hope, self-esteem, lack and fear. Become skillful with your money. In that way, you will not be easy pickings for Manipulators. A person skillful with his or her money is stronger. Start your studies and make your plans today.

8. How You Can Release the Brakes So You Really Succeed!

"How do I deal with the job interview question: 'What is one of your weaknesses?'"—asked one of my graduate students. I replied that one needs to talk about an "okay weakness."

What is that?

An "okay weakness" has these elements:

a) You sought instruction or coaching to help you improve.

b) You use a daily method to handle this weakness.

In a job interview, Mina said, "I've given this a lot of thought. At one time, I had a difficulty with prioritizing. So I took a time management workshop, and I learned about the 80/20 rule. The idea was that 80% of the best results come from 20% of what we do. So now, I have "80/20" on the screen of my smart phone. I also have a Post-it Note with '80/20' inscribed on it attached to the phone on my desk."

So talk about the coaching you've gained and your method to work on the weakness daily. In this way, you demonstrate that you're coachable and flexible, and you're a fast learner: ideal qualities for a new hire.

The big point is that the weakness is something you can work on and it is not a fixed characteristic.

What's a fixed characteristic? "Shy." "Bad with numbers." "Messy." "Disorganized."

When you want to make a leap forward in your career and in your life, use this pattern:

"Before now, I did not _____

and today, I'm going to _____."

Paul said: "Before now, I did not devote time to clear my desk, and today, I'm going to put in 15 minutes to clear my desk before I leave for the evening. "

When you let go of the tendency to give yourself disempowering labels (for a supposed characteristic), you'll find that your personal energy is enhanced. Why? A label is like fixing you to a wall. You're stuck and the situation is hopeless. That assessment drains personal energy. But the label is only a mental construct. Instead, choose to identify actions: an action that you failed to do and an action that you're choosing to do. Now, hope is restored and personal energy is enhanced.

For example, Alandra has a messy desk. But she is not a messy person. Her computer files are impeccably arranged on her laptop computer. Also, she devotes effort to her appearance and her wardrobe demonstrates style and grace. So she would benefit from the above pattern: "Before now, I did not _____, and today, I'm going to _____."

Be careful about the labels you say about yourself; the labels can turn into negative self-fulfilling prophesies. In effect, when you give yourself a label, you are programming your own thinking and behavior—which lead to the negative results you experience.

For example, I tell myself that I have an excellent memory. Recently, I contacted Lou Heckler, author of an audio program entitled Achieving Excellence that I heard more than 20 years ago. He was surprised to hear that I remembered his program for over 20 years, and I enjoyed telling him that I share one of his particular ideas with my current graduate students.

You see, this is an example that I emphasize to myself that I do have an excellent memory.

What do you want to emphasize about yourself? Are you insightful, trustworthy, creative . . .? Good for you!

Also, if you're in a job interview, you can use an "okay weakness."

As I mentioned, the "okay weakness" includes these elements:

a) you sought instruction or coaching to help you improve.

b) you use a daily method to handle this weakness.

How you describe yourself to others (and to yourself) is crucial to how much energy you have to take action on your own behalf. Guard your own feelings and energy level. Then, you'll open the doors wide for more success to flow in.

Some Thoughts about Labeling Yourself—and Persuasion and Seduction

What is a fast way to drain your energy? Give yourself a negative label. Then you're playing into the hands of a Manipulator. How? A negative label can drain your energy and then subconsciously, you might be metaphorically starving for some positive attention.

I once heard a friend say that she was "not that smart." That was a sad moment to me as her friend. It could be an indication of her low self-esteem. People with low self-esteem are particularly vulnerable to inappropriate persuasion or seduction. Why? Because they feel bad and long for someone's approval. Who will give them approval? A Manipulator.

My friend's comment is probably not even accurate. Why? Because she probably has high intelligence in areas that she's not even giving herself credit for. Psychologist Howard Gardner identified seven different types of intelligence:

1. Logical-mathematical intelligence
2. Bodily-kinesthetic intelligence
3. Visual-spatial intelligence
4. Interpersonal (or emotional) intelligence

5. Intrapersonal intelligence
6. Musical intelligence
7. Verbal-linguistic intelligence

[It has been suggested that there are other intelligences: #8 Naturalist Intelligence and #9 Existential Intelligence.]

It's important to be careful about giving yourself a negative label because such a label could become a negative self-fulfilling prophesy. I have met a number of people who say that they are not good at remembering names. And they get exactly that result. Why? Because they have programmed themselves to fail at remembering names.

On the other hand, when I'm memorizing student names, I give myself full credit. While taking attendance, I tell myself, "Yes! I've remembered 10 names so far! That's 10 to 2."

Build yourself up. This is your true defense against inappropriate persuasion or seduction.

9. How You Can Light a Candle when Things Look Dark—and Renew Your Energy

"I don't think I can handle this. It's just too much," Serena said to her friend Mara. Serena's elderly mother had, over the recent years, become more and more rigid and severe in her criticisms. Her boyfriend was pushing for them to move to another home. And finally, her supervisor was irritable each day, buckling under new pressure from his boss. Serena felt her energy drained and her spirit deflated.

Such stressful elements of life impinge on many of us. In order to make our dreams come true, we need to be skilled in how to bounce back from life's disappointments and tragedies. Here is the M.O.R.E. process to renew your energy:

M – Magnify the positive.

O – Open to nurturing.
R – Realize things change moment to moment.
E – Experience subtle shifts inside you.

1. Magnify the positive

Talk about anything that is positive with friends. Make a big deal about it. So many of us have been conditioned to complain and complain. Why? Because we've been mimicking the people near us since childhood.

Researchers note that repeated complaining does not accomplish the release of negative emotions; instead, repeated complaining keeps a person in a negative space. Find little things to be grateful for. Start with the phrase "I am grateful for . . ." You can bring this phrase to mind at various points in your daily life. My clients say: "My laptop computer works"; "My car started up this morning" . . . They affirm these positive details to themselves and to friends.

2. Open to nurturing

Wouldn't it be great if the world would respond just the way we prefer—and exactly in our preferred timeframe? Yes, it would be great. But we can't count on it happening. In other words, the world does not have nurturing us as a priority. So we must become experts at nurturing ourselves. Pick something that brightens your day. Perhaps, you enjoy painting a picture or listening to music. Just 10 minutes of doing something pleasant will brighten your whole day.

3. Realize things change moment to moment

One day while we were doing errands, my sweetheart mentioned a chore that I needed to do and I checked with how I was feeling. Drained, tired. So I said, "I'll see how I'm feeling when we get home." I reached into the glove compartment for a nutritional bar. After I ate the nutritional bar I felt better. And I was able to complete the task on entering my home. My point is that my mood changed after I fortified my personal energy. Another example: when a family member says, "There won't be parking in front of that store," my response is, "We'll see." And, we usually find parking quickly!

4. Experience subtle shifts inside you

Take in a deep breath. Yes, right now. And gently let the air flow out. Repeat this three times and you'll probably notice that you feel better. You're feeling better—even if your to-do list didn't get any smaller. Deep breathing or taking a walk near trees (perhaps a local park) or water, helps us feel grounded and centered.

Imagine that the above methods are part of your *Low Mood Tool Kit*. The Kit is a list of what you can do to feel some relief. "Chocolate!" is my sweetheart's favorite Kit element. Keep the list in your wallet or purse.

I also keep a list of my goals (and what I'm looking forward to) with me at all times. The lists relate to both relief and inspiration. These are two powerful elements so that you "light a candle" and dispel the darkness of fatigue or temporary downheartedness.

Light a candle today.

Some Thoughts about "Light a Candle"—and Persuasion and Seduction

If you don't light your own candle, you'll probably find that your life is merely one of work and drudgery. Such an attitude will make you vulnerable to inappropriate persuasion or seduction. Why? Because a human being who feels overwhelmed and downhearted is hurting. In such a state, people tend to hunger for approval. And, if you fail to be nice to yourself, you'll be hungry for kindness from just about anyone. A Manipulator can take advantage of this situation. Don't let this happen. Become the expert of nurturing yourself. It's your best defense.

How can you empower yourself on a daily basis? Make sure that you have something joyful every day — and take 10 seconds to write down a note in your daily journal. In my book *10 Seconds to Wealth: Master the Moment Using Your Divine Gifts*, I cite the research that has uncovered that people need to focus for 10 seconds. Why? Because 10 seconds is the duration that it takes for something positive to impact your long-term memory. This is not trivial. We're talking about conditioning your brain to be inclined toward the strong and the positive.

10. How You Can Handle Tough Moments — and Protect Your Day

Have you ever had a friend respond to you and say, "Wow! It sounds like you've had a bad day"?

One year, I received a tough phone call from my father. He explained that he was calling from a hospital and that my mother had required an ambulance to get her there. [We live in different parts of California.] I experienced some really tough moments of worrying. I packed as fast as I could, preparing to be in my parents' city and visit for hours over a succession of days. I said to my sweetheart, "I'm preparing for a 'siege.'"

Was that a bad day? I would call it "a day with tough moments in it."

How is "bad day" versus "a day with tough moments in it" an important difference? It is about how you use your brain. That is, "having a bad day" is a blanket statement, and it puts a damper on the whole day. For example, I have a friend who deals with her clinical depression. Is she a "depressed person"? She has decided to reframe the situation by saying: "I'm a person dealing with depression symptoms." She tells me that she is a person first—and that she is a spiritual being.

My point here is that your brain is a powerful organ that can help you . . . or hold you back.

A negative blanket statement can drain you of vital energy. Why? The negative blanket statement puts you into an unresourceful state of being. You won't be able to see possible solutions. And that drains energy. Things stay bad and they may get worse. Some people start with an argument at home in the morning and have further arguments with co-workers that same day.

Instead, I invite you to consider the phrase: "a day with tough moments in it."

When I look through my personal diary, I notice at least 97% of my days are "good days"—with some days having "tough moments." I purposely make decisions and take actions so that a few tough moments do not poison my whole day. For example, this morning, I woke up with thoughts, that is, memories, of really mean words that a relative said yesterday. I told myself "Just one more thought" to remind myself that I could switch the direction of my thoughts. I can think about something better than yesterday's unpleasantness.

So I crawled out of bed and started my day reading something positive, calling some friends, and preparing for doing work that would uplift the hearts of clients and students.

Remember, "Just one more thought" and invite yourself to make a brand new day into something that enriches your life.

There is so much in life that we do not control: someone else's behavior, someone else's approval or even if a person will be courteous.

We can influence ourselves into a positive direction with what we focus on . . . and with what we decide to do in the next moment.

I remember one year when I had severe back pain due to some sort of strain. Even then, I noticed that the intensity of the pain varied moment-to-moment. A friend asked, "How are you doing, Tom?" I replied, "Making the most of this moment."

My point here is that I avoided the blanket statement of "a bad day." I take each moment as it comes. In this way, I have more chances to enjoy more of the day.

Some Thoughts about "Protecting Your Day"—and Persuasion and Seduction

Once you pronounce a day as a "bad day" you're vulnerable to the machinations of a Manipulator. Why? Because you're hurting and you're looking for some relief. Let's say you have an argument with your romantic partner in the morning. Then a truly attractive client stops by your office. Now, you're basking in that person's approval. You might be tempted to accept a lunchtime get-together.

Instead, make a conscious choice to identify an argument as a few tough moments. Then, as you go through the rest of your day, remind yourself that those few moments do not necessarily color your whole day. Be good to yourself. Perhaps, listen to music or take a walk in a local park. Bring a smile to your own face.

Remember, you have a significant "handle" on how your day turns out. The handle is the direction of your thoughts. There's an old phrase, "Don't go there"—and that can be a switchphrase for you. A switchphrase helps you switch the direction of your thoughts. I find it helpful to memorize some powerful switchphrases (and then repeat them to myself, depending on the situation):

- "This is not a teaching moment" (This helps me avoid giving advice to unreceptive people.)
- "I'm grateful for . . ."
- "I don't run that show" (This helps me avoid taking on too much inappropriate work.)

When you effectively use switchphrases, you can protect your day from falling into the disempowering thought of "a bad day." Choose to focus your thoughts in an empowering direction. If your thoughts stray toward negative judgments, gently bring them back to a positive focus. I always remember something Richard Carlson, author of *Don't Sweat the Small Stuff*, said to me: "It's not that I don't get stressed out. I've just learned to spend much less time there."

Stay strong.

Conclusion to Use Strategies to Make Yourself Stronger (Your Defense Against Manipulators)

When you make yourself stronger, you have the power to defend yourself from a Manipulator's tactics.

In summary, here are *Ten Strategies to Make Yourself Stronger:*

1. When confronted with criticism, go "neutral."

2. If you feel triggered, devote some time to change your pattern and create an Empowering Trigger Sequence.

3. When someone offers advice, ask yourself: "Do I know what my heart wants? Does this advice apply to that? Will this advice support my personal vision?"

4. About approval . . . Live your life expressing your "aliveness" and creativity. When approval happens to arrive, enjoy it. We can make approval into something that we prefer instead of something that we try to "demand"

from life. Approval from others really is like an occasional dessert.

5. Guard your own flame of life. Ask yourself these questions:
- Does this build me up?
- Is this tearing me down?
- Does this help me do something positive (with integrity) with my life?
- Does this give me strength?
- Does this drain my energy?

6. When you want to ask for support, practice coming up with a "Turnaround." For example, turn around "Nobody helps me around here until I yell" into "I'd really appreciate some help. Would you rather take out the garbage or put some oil on the squeaky hinge on the backdoor?"

7. To accept an opportunity to earn more money, you'll probably need to press through fear. Get coaching and rehearse what you might say in a job interview or a pitch meeting with a potential client (as examples).

8. Stop giving yourself disempowering labels. Instead say to yourself, "Before now, I did not do _____(verb), and today, I'm going to _____(verb)." That is, set a plan of action.

9. Light a candle when things look dark; start with the phrase "I am grateful for . . ."

10. Avoid labeling a day as a "bad day"; consider that your day is a good day with some tough moments in it. Then, focus on each present moment. Make the best of each moment as it arrives.

These methods take practice. And they're worth it because you are worth it. And the only person to ensure that your life gets better is you.

Now, I'm going to complete this section with two guest

articles. In the first one Dr. Elayne Savage guides us to strengthen our responses to other people.

* * *

Taking Back Your Power
by Dr. Elayne Savage

Allison knew she had to say something to her boss—and soon. That woman was running all over her. Breathing down her neck. Micromanaging everything she did.

Allison couldn't breathe.

And the worst part was she was taking the interactions between the two of them so personally. Dwelling, fretting, ruminating took up most of her day. Her productivity was suffering

Most recently Allison's boss insisted she rewrite a proposal three times. All the changes were minor and probably nonessential. The requested revisions were time-consuming and tedious. Allison resented them. And the resentment was interfering with her relationships with everyone in the office.

Lost Time and Productivity

Isn't it amazing how resentments like these take up so much emotional space? And, resentments can interfere with your ability to do work and connect with co-workers. Think of the lost time and performance and productivity resulting from all the stewing and dwelling.

But to Allison, the thought of speaking up sends fear waves up her spine. What if she looks like a fool? What if her concerns are dismissed as trivial? Or she is criticized or even ridiculed? Or her boss uses her concerns as an example to team members and makes her out to be 'wrong and bad.'

Allison feels intimidated because, bottom line, she fears

rejection.

That's where I could help out when Allison consulted me about how to not take things so personally and create a more productive work situation.

As a communication coach I guided Allison in how to get past the fear and dread of confronting a situation. I taught her the skills to communicate clearly, directly and effectively.

We looked at how her early history might play a role in her hesitancy to be direct. It only took a short time for Allison to connect her present timidity to the spoken (as well as unspoken) 'rules' her father set out: "It's not OK to question authority. Just do as you are told. Or else!"

Allison had been hinting around, hoping her boss would read her mind. We strategized how to be direct. We focused on being able to separate the act of confronting a situation from the act of confronting a person. There is a huge difference, but most of us confuse the two.

We practiced do-able ways to say what she needs to say to her boss. It took a few tries to arrive at a statement that feels relatively comfortable to her:

She came up with "I would really appreciate it if _____."

Allison also felt fairly at ease saying something like "I can (revise the proposal) or I can (make the calls you asked me to make). Which would you like me to do first?"

Romantically Speaking

But it's not only work situations that can feel controlling. Romantic relationships can be daunting as well. Friendships too.

Hannah has been feeling trapped for two years. Her charming, witty sometimes loving husband also puts her down with demeaning verbal remarks—sometimes in front of others. Then comes the honeymoon period when he is loving. He says, "Nobody will ever love you like I love you."

She was so confused by his behavior. Each time these exchanges took place, Hannah felt more unlovable.

But then it was so familiar. Her mother used to tease her, make fun of her developing figure and tell her she was not as pretty or as smart as the other girls at school.

The message Hannah brought to her adult years was, "People who love me also hurt me."

Bullying Behavior

When a friend or lover or boss is a bully, it creates an even more complicated situation. Bullying usually involves repeated incidents intended to intimidate, offend, degrade or humiliate. Bullies feel they have the right to mistreat someone and they won't be held accountable for their actions. Look for a pattern of incidents as well as the severity of the behavior. Sometimes bullying takes the more subtle form of manipulation.

It's important to remember that bullies chose victims based on the bully's own insecurities. Bullies, in the act of bullying, are really puffing themselves up because they feel small inside.

Bullying in the workplace takes many forms. Here are just a few:

 - harassing, intimidating, excluding or isolating, spreading rumors

 - constantly changing work guidelines

 - assigning unreasonable duties or establishing impossible deadlines that are set-ups for failure

You can imagine the high cost of bullying in the workplace including lost productivity, absenteeism, stress-related illnesses and sick time.

Bullying in personal situations can take the form of:

- Demeaning, critical, belittling, insulting, accusatory comments

- Physical, emotional or sexual harassment or abuse

- Unreasonable demands or pressure to do uncomfortable behavior(s)

- Restricting your friendships or social contacts

The toll on the relationship and the family is immense. Research shows the long-term effect of emotional or physical domestic violence on children can be similar to the effect of direct emotional or physical abuse of the child.

What can you do?

Experts say the best defense against a bully is taking action—any kind of action. Provide clear examples of the bullying behavior. Firmly tell the person that his or her behavior is unacceptable. Ask them to stop.

If it's a work situation, consider putting a description of the bullying behavior and a warning to stop in writing with a copy to the bully's supervisor. If the bully is your supervisor, send the memo to Human Resources or an upper management person in the company.

Personal bullying situations can follow the same strategy: Describe the behavior, make a clear statement that it is unacceptable, and ask them to stop. When there is inappropriate behavior, there needs to be consequences. State them clearly and follow through.

Realize you cannot change your partner. You can, however, change your reaction to your partner's behavior.

Get professional help, couples counseling or relationship coaching.

For help with protecting yourself from an emotionally or physically abusive relationship and learning resources, call the National Domestic Violence Hotline:

http://www.thehotline.org/get-help/help-in-your-area/

1-800-799-SAFE (7233)

It Ain't Much But It's Home

What are the messages we develop as children that affect our adult work and personal relationships?

Some of us learn that it isn't OK to say 'no' to someone. If we did, we might disappoint them. We might lose their approval or even their love. So we learn to 'go along to get along.'

We come to fear that if we stand up for ourselves, they might withdraw their love, totally reject us or even abandon us. This thought is unnerving when we depend on that person. So we go through life trying to protect people from hurt feelings and end up hurting ourselves in the process.

Often the result is we feel victimized and resentful when, in fact, we are turning our power over to the other person.

Some of us can't look out after our own needs because we honestly don't know what our needs are. As children we are so busy looking out for other people's needs, we don't realize we have needs of our own. To us, needs feel like neediness. And it's surely not OK to be needy!

As children, we never learned to state needs directly; as adults we don't have a clue how to go about it.

One way to nurture your sense of self and independence is to recognize and honor your needs.

Here is an exercise I suggest to my coaching and therapy clients, although for many, this is very difficult at first:

Each day upon awakening ask yourself:
- "What would make me feel good today?"
- "What do I want? What do I need?"
- "From whom?" (Yourself? Someone else?)
- "In what way? What form would it take?"

You might also ask yourself how you would know your

want or need is met. Defining these needs, putting words to them, may be a brand new experience for you because no one gave you permission to do it before.

Don't be surprised if you struggle with it at first. Try to have patience and keep practicing. Doing this exercise regularly could change your perspective on life. Practice checking in with yourself throughout the day about how you feel and what would make you feel better. You will develop a more defined sense of yourself and new respect for both yourself and your needs.

In work or personal situations, saying clearly and directly what you need inputs you in a proactive role. It is more effective than complaining, which puts you in a 'victim' role. What works best is to describe how you want the interaction to go next time. Step-by-step. Folks can always use a how-to guide!

Create Your Own How-to Guide

If you find yourself involved in a controlling relationship, you develop specialized skills that help you survive through this crisis situation.

A good way to transform crisis into opportunity is to survey the past and ask yourself, "What can I learn from this that I can use in the present and perhaps carry into the future with me?"

This attitude allows you to develop a new approach to life where you can see things from a different perspective and make new choices.

One coaching client summed it up: "I can read people and their moods really well. I can size up people and situations. I'm flexible. I can get along with people. I sure learned a lot about looking and listening when I was in that relationship. In fact, I'm an expert!"

Dr. Elayne Savage, is known as The Queen of Rejection.®

She is a workplace coach, psychotherapist, speaker and author. An expert on how not to take rejection and disappointment so personally, she teaches and consults on developing effective communication skills. Her relationship books, *Breathing Room—Creating Space to Be a Couple* and *Don't Take It Personally! The Art of Dealing with Rejection* have been published in 9 languages.

Website: http://www.QueenofRejection.com

Blog: http://TipsFromTheQueenOfRejection.com

Now, we turn to specific methods that persuaders use. I noticed that top PR professionals must be quite persuasive or they do not succeed in placing articles or gaining TV show appearances for their clients. Here is my interview with Danek S. Kaus.

An Interview with Danek S. Kaus,
author of *You Can Be Famous! Insider Secrets to Getting Free Publicity*

Tom: Dan, when I read your book, I noticed that a lot of details that you recommend for an author to connect with journalists apply to how a persuader connects with a new person.

Dan: First, I come from the point of view that my reader has a positive message to communicate.

Tom: I hear you about that. You have a section called "Know Your Quarry."

Dan: Yes. I write about how opportunities for publicity in the media are all around you. The most obvious outlets are newspapers, magazines, and TV and radio stations. Within each of those categories are many different offerings. Each has its own audience and needs.

Tom: And so, a persuader is going to do some form of research to get to know the background on someone before they meet on the phone or some other way.

Dan: Yes. In my business, we write a press release. One thing I emphasize in my book is that The Headline is the Most Important Part of the News Release! A good headline will make the reporter want to learn more and continue reading. The first paragraph is crucial to the success of your release. It should be just a few sentences that explain or backup the headline. The main idea or hook should be the first sentence or two of this paragraph. It's called the lead.

Tom: And it seems to me: a person crafting a press release has done some research to make sure that the headline will compel a TV/radio producer to want to keep on reading the press release. A third detail I noticed is your emphasis on quotes in a press release.

Dan: Quotes liven up copy, so be sure to use them if you can. Many releases wrap up with a good quote that sums up the idea that is being pitched.

Tom: I also notice that effective persuaders use quotes to legitimize what they say. A persuader might say, "I was talking with Joe about the repairs I did. And he said, 'Mike, I can always count on you to do a great job and charge fair prices.'"

Dan: Yes. A quote is a powerful tool.

Tom: So here's an idea that occurs to me. I can actually sum up how a persuader influences a new person by adapting what a PR expert does for getting TV show interviews.

1. Know your quarry.
2. Craft a compelling headline.
3. Use quotes.

I notice that a persuader will often get the listener to believe something by citing corroborative evidence. The persuader will use quotes made by notable people.

Danek: True. There's something I want to add here about persuasion. It's not just about words or quotes. Neuro Linguistic Programming (NLP), among other things, studies the relationship between language and brain function. I have co-authored a book entitled Power Persuasion that discusses the methods of NLP.

NLP has determined that some people are primarily visually oriented (V). Others are more auditory (A). And some are more in touch with their physical feelings and emotions, or what is termed kinesthetic (K). From this, we get the term VAK. You can tell which sensory mode someone prefers to use by listening to the words they say.

Visuals think in pictures and the language they use reflects that. They might say, "I see what you mean," "I get the picture" or "That looks good to me." In a sales presentation, a Visual prospect might say, "Show me what you've got."

An Auditory might say, "That sounds good," "I hear what you're saying" or "That rings true." During a staff meeting, an Auditory might say, "Let me hear your idea."

A Kinesthetic will "Want to get a handle on something," "Try it on for size" or "Have a gut feeling." If you are making a proposal to a Kinesthetic, he or she might say, "Lay it on me."

The key then, to creating Instant Rapport with each of these types is to use language that they can understand and relate to. To do otherwise would be like going to Germany and refusing to speak German, even though you know the language.

If you say to an Auditory, "Do you see what I mean?" they won't. But if you ask, "Do you hear what I'm saying?" they probably will. Not only that, they're more likely to agree with you because you are speaking their language.

And when you speak their language, you create rapport. That's what a PR expert needs to do when first talking and interacting with a journalist or TV producer.

Tom: You mention rapport. Would you say more about it?

Danek: Creating rapport is critical to all human interaction, whether you are trying to sell something, make an appointment, close a deal or get a date, rapport creates a connection that makes persuasion possible.

Tom: How about creating rapport during a telephone call?

Danek: You create instant rapport on the phone by matching the voice characteristics of the person on the other end. You can match their speed, volume, and tonality. Let's take them one at a time.

Speed—you've probably noticed that people talk at different speeds. To create rapport, match the speed of your speech to theirs. You may have to hurry up to match that rapid-fire native of New York City, but you'll need to speak more slowly with that prospect from the deep south.

Volume—do they speak loudly and boldly or in a soft, almost whisper that you have to struggle to hear? Again, in creating instant rapport it is critical to behave like them.

Tonality—is the tone of their voice high or low? Whatever it is, do your best to match it.

Tom: It really impresses me that a PR expert needs to be a master of persuasion.

Danek: That's true. The PR expert must develop new skills. There's something important I want to share with you. I interviewed author Keith Harrell some years ago. And there are a number of things he said that I still remember.

"Attitude is involved in everything you do. It is the starting point and the stopping point of all success," he told me. In order to change your attitude, you must first stop the flow of negativity into the three "gates" of your mind and emotions.

The first is the ear gate. "We are bombarded with a lot of negative news and information. One way to change your attitude when you hear something negative is to say out loud something positive," Keith said.

Years ago, when Keith worked at a large corporation, they gathered hundreds of people together to announce that there would be layoffs. Knowing that there would be vacancies, Keith jumped to his feat and asked the speaker, "Can I get a bigger office?" This produced a lot of laughter and helped put a positive note into a very negative situation.

"I was able to look at other opportunities with a proactive attitude while other people were stuck in fear," Keith said.

As it turned out, he was one of those who was scheduled to be laid off. But because of his positive attitude, one of looking for new opportunities in any setback, he landed on his feet.

Tom: Powerful. It begins with attitude. You have to believe good things are possible for you.

Danek: I agree. Now, the second gate is the eye gate. In order to protect this gate, Keith said to avoid watching or reading the news first thing in the morning and before bed at night. "Read something positive that will renew your mind," Keith suggested.

You can renew your mind by reading inspirational books, your written list of goals or positive affirmations, which are statements about how you would like to be, written in the present tense. Keith advised putting these written statements all around your house and workplace so that you see them constantly. Every time you see one of your positive affirmations, it can have a dramatic impact on your attitude. The effect is cumulative. The more you see the affirmations, the more positive your attitude will be.

The third gate is your mouth. You must learn how to control what you say. "The mouth is the pen to the heart. Every word you think you are writing to the tablet of your heart," Keith told me. In order to increase confidence, speak like someone who is confident. "You never hear a champion or successful person say 'I just got lucky,'" Keith said.

According to him, attitude determines your feelings, and feelings determine your actions. "And it is your actions that determine your results," Keith said.

Tom: Danek, I'm glad you mentioned Keith. He passed away in October of 2010, but I'm currently reading and learning from his book Connect: Building Success, Through People, Purpose and Performance.

Danek: I'm sorry to hear that. He was a really nice guy. But, at least his words are still with us. That's the power of books.

Tom: Yes. I'm glad that I have a great team that helps me with my books.

Danek: I seem to recall that you wrote 36 books that are up on Amazon.com.

Tom (smiling): Yes. Thanks for that detail. And thanks for this interview. I've learned a lot from your book, You Can Be Famous! Insider Secrets to Getting Free Publicity.

The late **Danek S. Kaus** was an author, journalist, and publicist. Dan was also a produced screenwriter of an award-wining feature film.

* * *

To protect yourself from inappropriate persuasion and seduction, stay aware of the persuasion tools that Danek S. Kaus wrote about in his book:
1. Know your quarry
2. Craft a compelling headline.
3. Use quotes.

When I think of "craft a compelling headline," I'm

focusing on how a persuader or seducer formulates the exact thing to say to seize your attention. They often press hidden "hot buttons" on you.

Be sure to know your "hot buttons" (discussed earlier in this book) and to shore up your defenses.

When you strengthen yourself, you feel better. You enjoy peace because you know that you are prepared to ward off inappropriate persuasion or seduction.

A FINAL WORD AND SPRINGBOARD TO YOUR DREAMS

Congratulations on your efforts as your worked with the material in this book. To get even more value from this book, take the plans and insights that you created and place them in some form in your calendar or day planner. *Plan and take action.* Return to these pages again and again to reconnect with the material and take your life to higher levels.

The best to you,
Tom

Tom Marcoux
Executive Coach and Spoken Word Strategist

Special Offer Just for Readers of this Book:

Contact Tom Marcoux at tomsupercoach@gmail.com for special discounts on **coaching,** books, workshops and presentations. Just mention your experience with this book.

==> See an Excerpt from Tom Marcoux's book, *Darkest Secrets of Negotiation Masters*—on the next page.

An Excerpt from
Darkest Secrets of Negotiation Masters:
How to Protect Yourself, Overcome Intimidation, Get Stronger, and Turn the Power to Good
by Tom Marcoux, Executive Coach – Spoken Word Strategist
Copyright Tom Marcoux

BOOK I
Darkest Secrets of Negotiation Masters

I wasn't going to write this book, but something shocking happened that pushed me to write it—so you could learn how to protect yourself.

First, you need to know that for 27 years, I've been dedicated to helping people just like you. I've helped people protect themselves from physical danger. I started by teaching karate, and then swimming—and now communication methods for positive results.

The incident that pushed me to write this book occurred when someone I trusted to work on a deal for me turned against me. He wanted to do the least amount of work and wanted to "force me" to settle for an amount that didn't cover my expenses. How is this shocking? I've worked with this person on various projects, and I trusted him. This person wrote certain phrases in letters to me, which pushed me toward certain conclusions (like the negotiation is over; nothing else can be done) and disempowered me. In essence, he was "negotiating hard" and pushing me. (I will cover his dark methods and the countermeasures in the section "Entangle you in paperwork.")

I got angry. But I kept my calm on the outside. While upset, I realized that many people are getting hurt because Dark Negotiators are using techniques to coerce them into making poor decisions.

Now I can serve as your coach. You can learn about and rehearse the methods in this book so you can protect yourself and achieve favorable outcomes during negotiation.

Over the years, I have realized that not only do business people use intimidation and dark negotiation methods, so do some of our own family members. Within a number of paragraphs, I will show you *Countermeasures to 9 Dark Negotiation Methods.*

Before we go further, we must discuss how you can empower yourself.

You Can Turn a Negotiation into a Positive Process

What is negotiation? Some people talk of a negotiation as "a fight with words in which you're trying to defend yourself and then win." They also speak of the other person as "your opponent." This approach is misguided.

The Merriam-Webster Dictionary refers to "negotiation" as "the act or process of conferring with another so as to arrive at the settlement of some matter."

So this source does not define negotiation as "fighting with words." And in light of this, we can turn negotiation into a positive process. How? When necessary, we can calm down and think of the other person as simply "the other." When you make a positive connection with that person, you're more likely to negotiate a satisfying result. We avoid the trap of getting furious and considering the other person a villain. If you label the other person as a villain, what does that make you? It could make you a "hero". Or it could make you a "victim." Either way you shut yourself off from a powerful opportunity: you could turn the other person into an associate.

For example, I once turned "the other" in negotiation into an associate. It started off badly. This person was the manager of a store that was selling jewelry that was labeled

Sterling silver, but it turned my family member's finger green. In essence, the manager was part of an organization that was cheating. Still, I got this manager to give me what I wanted. How? I treated him as "the other" (just another person in front of me). That is, I consciously shifted my thoughts from "opponent" to the possibility of an associate to get the situation resolved. I appealed to his selfish interests. I realized that I could get what I wanted if I helped him get what he wanted. (Further into this book in the section Remember "It's All Good Practice," we go through a breakdown of the whole jewelry store negotiation.)

Now, I'll say something unusual:

Negotiation is often a crisis because it triggers and "floods" you with disempowering feelings.

When I use the phrase "triggers you," I'm talking about how something in the environment can bring up difficult emotions. For example, one of my clients grew up in a family that would yell during heated conversations. Her husband complains that she is "verbally abusive." The word "abusive" is a trigger for her: it reminds her of her father's bullying behavior. Now, she feels provoked, and her conversation with her husband escalates to an argument.

This book includes information from the field of neurology: the study of the brain....

End of Excerpt from
Darkest Secrets of Negotiation Masters

Purchase your copy of this book (paperback or ebook) at Amazon.com or BarnesandNoble.com
See **Free Chapters** of Tom Marcoux's 36 books at http://amzn.to/ZiCTRj

ABOUT THE AUTHOR

You want more and better, right? Imagine fulfilling your Big Dream.

Tom Marcoux can help you—in that he's coached thousands of people: CEOs, small business leaders, graduate students (at Stanford University) speakers, and authors.

Marcoux is known as an effective **Executive Coach** and **Spoken Word Strategist.**

(and Thought Leader—okay, writing 36 books helped with that!)

** *CEOs, Vice-Presidents, Other Executives, Small Business Leaders:*

You know that leading people and speaking at your best can be tough.

Marcoux solves problems while helping you amplify your own Charisma, Confidence and Control of Time.

Interested? Email Marcoux—tomsupercoach@gmail.com

Ask for a *Special Report:*

* 9 Deadly Mistakes to Avoid for Your Next Speech

** *Speakers, Experts—for a great TED Talk, Book, Audio Book, Speeches, YouTube Videos.*

Marcoux solve problems while helping you to make your

Concise, Compelling Message that gets people to trust you and get what you're offering (product, service, *an idea*).

Yes—the *San Francisco Examiner* designated Tom Marcoux as "The Personal Branding Instructor."

Marcoux is an expert on STORY. He won a Special Award at the EMMY AWARDS, and he directed a feature film that went to the CANNES FILM MARKET and earned international distribution.

(Marcoux helps you *be heard and be trusted*—a focus point of his 16th Anniversary edition book, *Connect: High Trust Communication for Your Success in Business and Life*.)

As a CEO, Marcoux leads teams in the United Kingdom, India and the USA. Marcoux guides clients & audiences (IBM, Sun Microsystems, etc.) in leadership, team-building, power time management and branding. See Tom's Popular BLOG: www.TomSuperCoach.com

Specialties: coach to CEOS * Executives * Small Business owners * Leaders * Speakers * Experts * Authors * Academics

One of his *Darkest Secrets* books rose to #1 on Amazon.com Hot New Releases in Business Life (and in Business Communication). A member of the National Speakers Association for over 15 years, he is a professional coach and guest expert on TV, radio, and print.

Marcoux addressed National Association of Broadcasters' Conference six years running. With a degree in psychology, Tom is a guest lecturer at **Stanford University**, DeAnza, & California State University, and teaches business communication, designing careers, public speaking, science fiction cinema/literature and comparative religion at Academy of Art University. He is engaged in book/film projects *Crystal Pegasus* (children's) and *Jack AngelSword* (thriller-fantasy). See Tom's well-received blogs

at www.BeHeardandBeTrusted.com

at www.YourBodySoulandProsperity.com

Consider engaging **Tom Marcoux as your Executive Coach.**

"As Tom's client for many years, I have benefited from

his wisdom and strategic approach. Do your career and personal life a big favor and get his books and engage him as **your Executive Coach.**" – Dr. JoAnn Dahlkoetter, author of *Your Performing Edge* and Coach to CEOs and Olympic Gold Medalists

"Tom Marcoux coached me to get more done in 10 days than other coaches in 2 years." – Brad Carlson, CEO of MindStrong LLC

As the Spoken Word Strategist, Tom Marcoux can help you with **speech writing** and **coaching for your best performance.**

As Tom says, *Make Your Speech a Pleasant Beach.*

Join Tom's Linkedin.com group: *Executive Public Speaking and Communication Power.*

At Google+: join the community "Create Your Best Life – Charisma & Confidence"

Get a **Free** report: "9 Deadly Mistakes to Avoid for Your Next Speech and 9 Surefire Methods" at

http://tomsupercoach.com/freereport9Mistakes4Speech.html

Tom Marcoux has trained CEOs, small business owners, and graduate students to speak with impact and gain audiences' tremendous approval and cooperation. *Learn how to present and get thunderous applause!*

"Tom, Thanks for your coaching and work with me on revising my speech at a major university. Working with you has been so enlightening for me. Through your gentle prodding and guidance I was able to write a speech that connects with the audience. I wish everyone could experience the transformation I have undergone. You have helped me discover the warm and compelling stories that now make my speech reach hearts and uplift minds. This was truly an empowering experience. I cannot thank you enough for your great assistance." — J.S.

"Tom Marcoux has been an NAB Conference favorite [speaker] for six years. And he is very energetic."

– John Marino, Vice President, National Association of Broadcasters, Washington, D.C.

"Using just one of Tom Marcoux's methods, I got more done in 2 weeks than in 6 months."

– Jaclyn Freitas, M.A.

Tom's Coaching features innovations:
- Dynamic Rehearsal
- Power Rehearsal for Crisis
- The Charisma Advantage that Saves You Time

Become a fan of Tom's graphic novels/feature films:
- Fantasy Thriller: *Jack AngelSword*
  type "JackAngelSword" at Facebook.com
- Science fiction: *TimePulse*
  www.facebook.com/timepulsegraphicnovel
- Children's Fantasy: *Crystal Pegasus*
  www.facebook.com/crystalpegasusandrose

See **Free Chapters** of Tom Marcoux's 36 books at http://amzn.to/ZiCTRj   Amazon.com

Your Notes:

www.ingramcontent.com/pod-product-compliance
Lightning Source LLC
Chambersburg PA
CBHW071313110426
42743CB00042B/1484